WINGS OVER WING

The story of a World War II Bomber Training Unit

by

Michael Warth

Also by Michael Warth
Great Brickhill in the Mid 1860's.

First published October 2001 by
The Book Castle
12 Church Street
Dunstable
Bedfordshire LU5 4RU

ISBN 1 903747 05 8

Typeset & Designed by Priory Graphics,
Flitwick, Bedfordshire.
Printed by Impress Print,
Corby, Northants.

CONTENTS

(Contents continued) Page

ACKNOWLEDGEMENTS

I would like to express my grateful thanks to all those who contributed towards making this book possible, to individuals for anecdotes, photographs and documents (key to credits as initials below), to the staff of the RAF Museum, Hendon and the Public Records Office at Kew, to INTERCOM and AIRCREW magazines. I am particularly indebted to the following for their help:

George Bignell (G.Bi.) – for many fascinating discussions (now sadly deceased).
Geoffrey Bond (G.Bo.) – for kindly allowing me access to initial research by his late brother Peter.
Fred Capron (F.C.) – for fabulous detail and enormous encouragement.
Ian Coleman (I.C.) – for access to his great knowledge of all matters RAF and unique photographs
Tony Lack (T.L.) – for proofreading and great encouragement.
Bob Soutar (B.S.) – for a wealth of information and photographs.

Thanks also to the following for their fascinating anecdotes and memories that have proved so invaluable in piecing the story together:

Don Abercrombie
Ken Annable
Rex Austen
Jack Bate (J.Ba.)
J.H.Berry
John Boxall (J.Bo.)
Denise Cramp
Denis Down
Harry George
Bruce Giles
Joan Greenacre
Allan Hardwicke
Jeffrey Harrington
Keith Hopkins
Len Land
Sam Lawton
Jack Lunn
Hugh Lynch-Blosse
Harry McLean
Keith McLean
Ken Meen
John Poynter (J.P.)
Dick Revill
Hugh Richards
Pat Richards
Brian Riley
Jack Robinson (J.R.)
Lewis Shaw
Johnny Silvester
Cliff Stewart
Ron Stotter
John Streeter
Donald Sykes
Don Taylor
Eric Taylor
John Thornton
Desmond Truss
Jack Warwick (J.W.)
John Whitworth

Thanks are also due to the following who have contributed in a variety of ways:

Tony Barker
Alec Bird
Jim Brookbank
David Collyer
T.Cooksey
Mr Cranwell
Alvin Fast
Eoin Ferris
Joyce Haynes
Val Hill (V.H.)
R.F.Jones
James Norris (J.N.)
J.Paton (J.Pa.)
Stephen Ramsden
Arthur Read
Derek Sadler (D.S.)
Maureen Thomas (M.T.)
R.P.Todd
Mr Warren

I must also thank my wife Julie and children Emily, Edward and Jonathan for their patience and encouragement.

ABOUT THE AUTHOR

Michael Warth was born in Reading in 1953 and after leaving school in 1971 completed teacher training at the Milton Keynes College Of Education. After a short period teaching in his home town, he took up a post at High Ash School in Great Brickhill, Buckinghamshire and his interest in local history led to the publication of his first book entitled "Great Brickhill In The Mid 1860's."

In 1984 Michael moved to Overstone School in Wing, eventually becoming Deputy Headteacher, a position he still holds today. Curiosity about a group of dilapidated buildings in fields near the village led to some local research which developed further as contact was made with former personnel who had been at RAF Wing during its relatively short existence. It soon became apparent that here was a story worth telling, of an establishment largely forgotten, which touched the lives of hundreds of men and women.

The result is "Wings Over Wing" which draws together facts and figures and vivid personal memories to give an insight into a small contributor to the nation's war machine in those heady days of World War II.

The badge of 26 Operational Training Unit bearing the motto 'Ala Minans' which is translated as 'the threat of wings.'

INTRODUCTION

Travelling today along the quiet, country lane from Wing to Cublington it is difficult to picture how different the scene was for those few years in the 1940's when events of wartime brought a level of activity previously unknown to this peaceful corner of rural England.

My own interest was aroused partly by the existence of a few dilapidated buildings amidst the fields and partly by the addresses of a few children in the school at which I teach – such as Bungalow 3, Wing Airfield.

An airfield at Wing? What sort of airfield? There's nothing there now is there? These were questions that went through my mind for a number of years until eventually my curiosity overcame me and I decided to find out more.

Through discussions with a few local people I was able to begin following a line of enquiry which linked all the parts together – the buildings, the airfield, the people.

From modest beginnings I then embarked on a project which brought me in touch with some of those whose lives were affected by their involvement in activities at RAF Wing. Those who went on to experience so much during the War, and indeed after it, still had vivid memories of the months or years spent there – most were happy, some were sad, all were nothing less than fascinating. What became clear was that this comparatively small and shortlived establishment had a story to tell, a story that deserved to be told, one that might simply be lost as the years passed by.

It soon became evident that here was a story of great courage and comradeship, where such strong bonds were formed between individuals and where groups of people had faith in each other, yet there were also elements of great sadness as such ties were broken by the ravages of war.

What follows is an attempt to reconstruct events at just one of a number of bomber training units or OTUs. Each had its part to play and each has its own story to tell, but much of the routine found at Wing will find accord with those who trained elsewhere.

The stories told by 'those who were there' are backed up by factual records and documents and augmented by photographs and illustrations, with the aim of giving some insight into life at such an establishment in the extraordinary days of World War II.

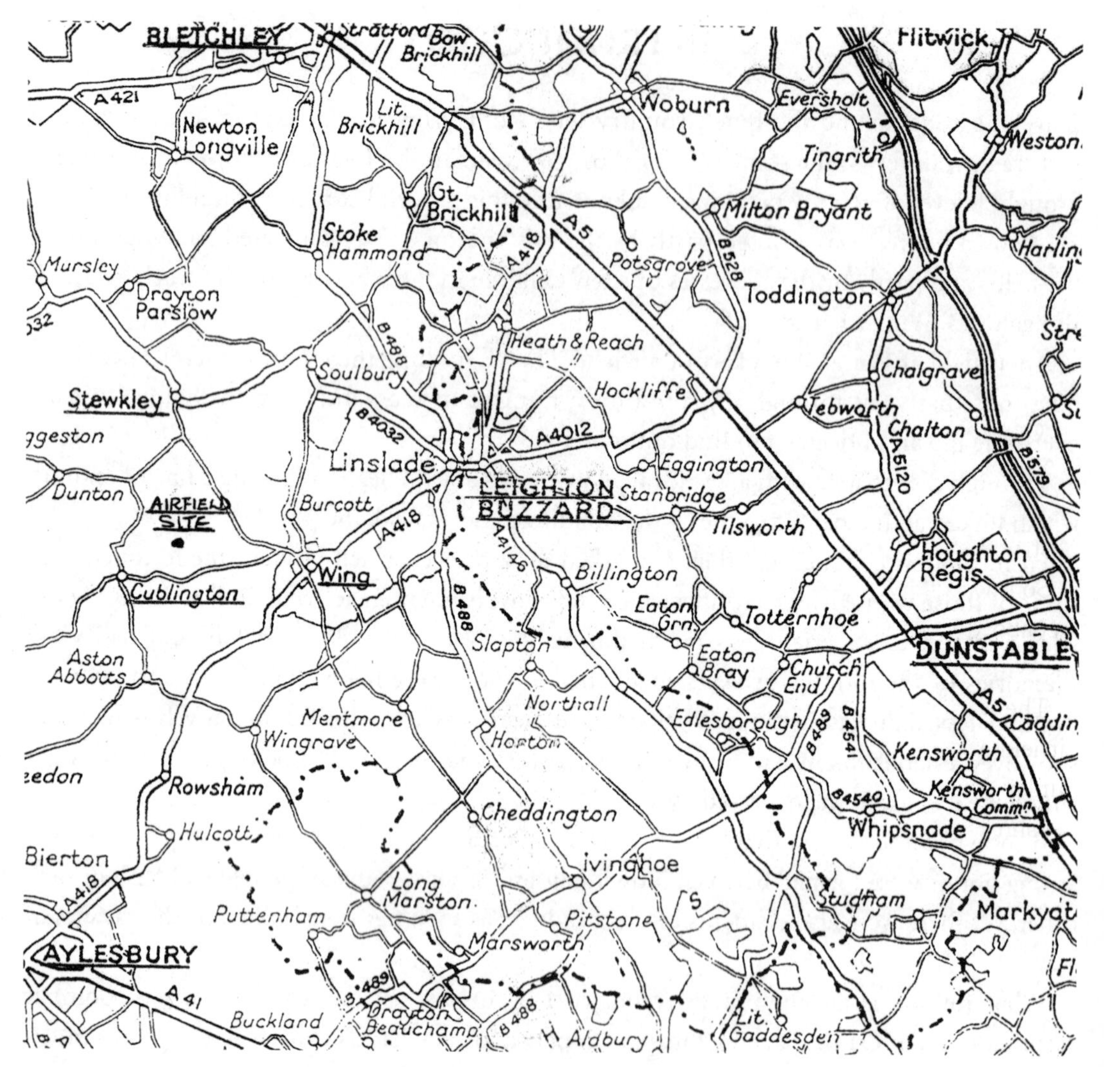

A map of Wing and its surrounding area, including Stewkley and Cublington.

CHAPTER 1
Early Days

The origins of RAF Station, Wing could be said to date from 1939 for it was in that year that the Air Ministry formed what was called the 'Aerodrome Board'. The function of the Board was to seek sites for the building of new airfields in order to meet the increasing demand for the training of pilots and aircrew.

The sites selected were required to be a minimum of 50 feet above sea level to eliminate the risk of flooding, but also had to be below 650 feet above sea level to avoid problems related to mist and fog.

When such a site was found and if it was free from obstructions it would be marked off on an OS map with a 1000 yard circle. This area would then be inspected for any minor obstructions and the proposed runway walked out.

So it was that in 1940 the site at Wing was selected on an area of relatively flat land some 140 feet above sea level and with no threat from hills or other obstructions. Its position was between the Wing to Cublington and Wing to Stewkley roads on Church land forming part of Glebe Farm.

The Air Ministry had already decided that the Station would function as a bomber training airfield and during the year construction began with the work being carried out by Bernard Sunley & Company.

John Thornton who was 14 at the time and working on the nearby Mount Pleasant Farm recalls,

> 'November witnessed feverish runway laying with the grotesque earth moving monsters working day and night whilst the massive concrete mixing machinery was stopped only by heavy frost.'

Another youngster to have witnessed the construction of the airfield was Arthur Read, who now farms land that once housed airfield buildings. On the same land then farmed by his father he remembers how,

> 'Most of the local farmers provided horses and carts to assist with the fetching and carrying of building materials.'

To maximise the output of trained crews,each parent airfield such as RAF Wing had a satellite airfield at which certain elements of the training programme were to be based. The satellite for Wing was RAF Cheddington, situated to the South of the village, adjacent to the road to Long Marston.

RAF Wing eventually opened on 17th November 1941, being initially occupied by an advanced party of 75 but it was not until the 2nd December that Group Captain J.N.D.Anderson arrived to take command of the newly built airfield.

The Station developed rapidly, with a variety of personnel being posted to Wing before the

Aerial view of RAF Wing taken 12.8.47 from 14,000 feet. Wing village is towards the bottom left corner, whilst Stewkley is top right. (G.Bo.)

end of the year, including numerous officers and over 400 airmen and on 15th January 1942 Operational Training Unit (OTU) number 26 was formed as part of No 7 (Training) Group Bomber Command.

On that date the Operations Record Book (ORB) states,

> 'This Station ceased to use the title of RAF Station, Wing on becoming 26 OTU.'

Denise Cramp was a WAAF who was at Wing from March 1942 and recalls,

> 'When I arrived the station was still under construction, with the workers, who were mainly Irish immigrants, living in huts near the Station HQ. Soon after the work was finished the huts were burnt down.'

Although construction work was continuing, by March the runways at Wing were still not yet fully cleared of obstructions. In the circumstances a decision was made to move headquarters to the satellite station at Cheddington in order that training could commence.

On the 15th 121 personnel arrived at Cheddington followed a week later by the first aircraft, four Ansons for flying training.

The first flight from Cheddington is recorded on the 26th March when an Anson conveyed instructors on liaison duties with other OTUs. Instructional training soon followed with the arrival of six Wireless Operator/Air Gunners and 12 Observers, the latter for training as navigators or bomb aimers, whilst on the 25th April, Number 1 Flying Training Course officially commenced with eight Ansons and Wellingtons for conversion flying.

Meanwhile, back at Wing, the runways had at last been made ready and Group Captain S.M.Park, who had assumed command in January, enjoyed the privilege of being first to land an aircraft, when the Tiger Moth he was piloting touched down on 18th March. Exactly one week later the ORB records the first accident at the airfield, when a Blenheim from RAF Odiham suffered slight damage when taxying. Thankfully there were no injuries reported on this occasion, although accidents at this and other OTUs became an all too frequent occurrence during their existence.

In May 26 OTU saw its first involvement with Operational Flying when both crews and aircraft were involved in the initial 1000 Bomber Raids over German cities. Full details of the contribution made by the training unit are dealt with in a later chapter, but it was undoubtedly an incredibly tense and busy time for all.

Training of course continued with five Flights now centred at Wing - A Flight involved flying training in Ansons, B, C and D concentrated on Operational Training and E Flight, newly formed in July, covered Air Firing.

Further developments occurred during the year which affected 26 OTU, the first of which was reorganisation within the RAF that resulted in the disbanding of No 7 Group. Following this, 26 OTU fell under the control of No 92 Group Bomber Command whose HQ was at Winslow Hall.

Even more significant however was the decision to cease training at Cheddington. This resulted from concerns over safety, as it became evident that hills and other obstructions in the vicinity of the airfield were a hazard that may have been,in part, responsible for accidents that had occurred in the short time since training began.

From September 1942 all activities were centred on Wing whilst RAF Cheddington was handed over to the United States 8th Army Air Force, initially as an administration satellite but soon after as an active base for aircraft.

To compensate for the loss of Cheddington, a new satellite airfield was necessary and this built at Little Horwood, with it taking over the role 2rd September . Here A and B Flights were to concentrate on Basic Flying Training with E Flight working in parallel with these providing aspects of Gunnery Training. At Wing, the more Advanced Flying Training in C and D Flights would take place as well as certain elements of Ground Training.

Also at Little Horwood could be found the 92 Group Communications Flight.

ACW Joan Greenacre (nee Webdale) was a WAAF who arrived at Wing in September 1942 as an MT driver. She remembers that,

> 'The airfield (at Wing) was newly opened and still lacking in such things as electric lights on the perimeter track, dispersals and even the runway. This made a lot of work for the flare path people when there was night flying as they had to turn out numerous times to replace lamps that had been laid earlier but had been run over by aircraft. It was a nightmare driving round the 'drome at night until better lighting was finally installed, as the lights on our vehicles were very poor due to blackout restrictions.'

Wing and its new satellite at Little Horwood developed into busy thriving airfields with the former having somewhere in the region of a thousand personnel scurrying to and fro involved in their various activities, be they aircrew, instructors, ground crew or others involved in the myriad occupations necessary for the effective operation of a training station.

As Ted Sweet remarks in his book 'The Enemy Below'

> 'The station teemed with personnel - I had never seen such a crowded and busy RAF Camp. Aircrews were everywhere, coming and going. We were all bemused by the quantity of aircrews present and also the general business-like atmosphere'.

Throughout its lifetime 26 OTU trained hundreds of aircrew before they moved on to Operational Flying in Bomber Squadrons which was a considerable feat and an important contribution to the War effort.

Many other visitors came to Wing: RAF officials, lecturers in specialist fields and instructors covering all aspects of flying. One of the more unusual officials to visit is recorded in the ORB for 17th July 1942. Flight Lieutenant Thomas was officially titled Air Ministry Pigeon Officer and his visit was for the purpose of selecting a site for a pigeon loft so that,

> 'pigeons would be available for distress purposes to 'all crews flying on operations over the sea."

Jeffrey Harrington was posted to Wing as a Sergeant Navigator for training in May 1943 and recalls the plight of such pigeons.

> 'On some flights we carried homing pigeons for release over the sea. Poor creatures, they would be ejected in paper bags via the flare chute and would then have to disentangle themselves and fly all the way back to their loft. The object of the paper bag was to prevent the feathers being damaged by the slipstream, but I doubt the pigeons

appreciated the fact!'

The Map of the airfield depicts its layout as it was when the Unit closed down in March 1946. From its early days development clearly continued, with new sites, buildings and facilities constructed within its five year lifespan. Few of the buildings now remain, particularly on the actual airfield site, whilst those that still stand are in poor condition. A few of the buildings have

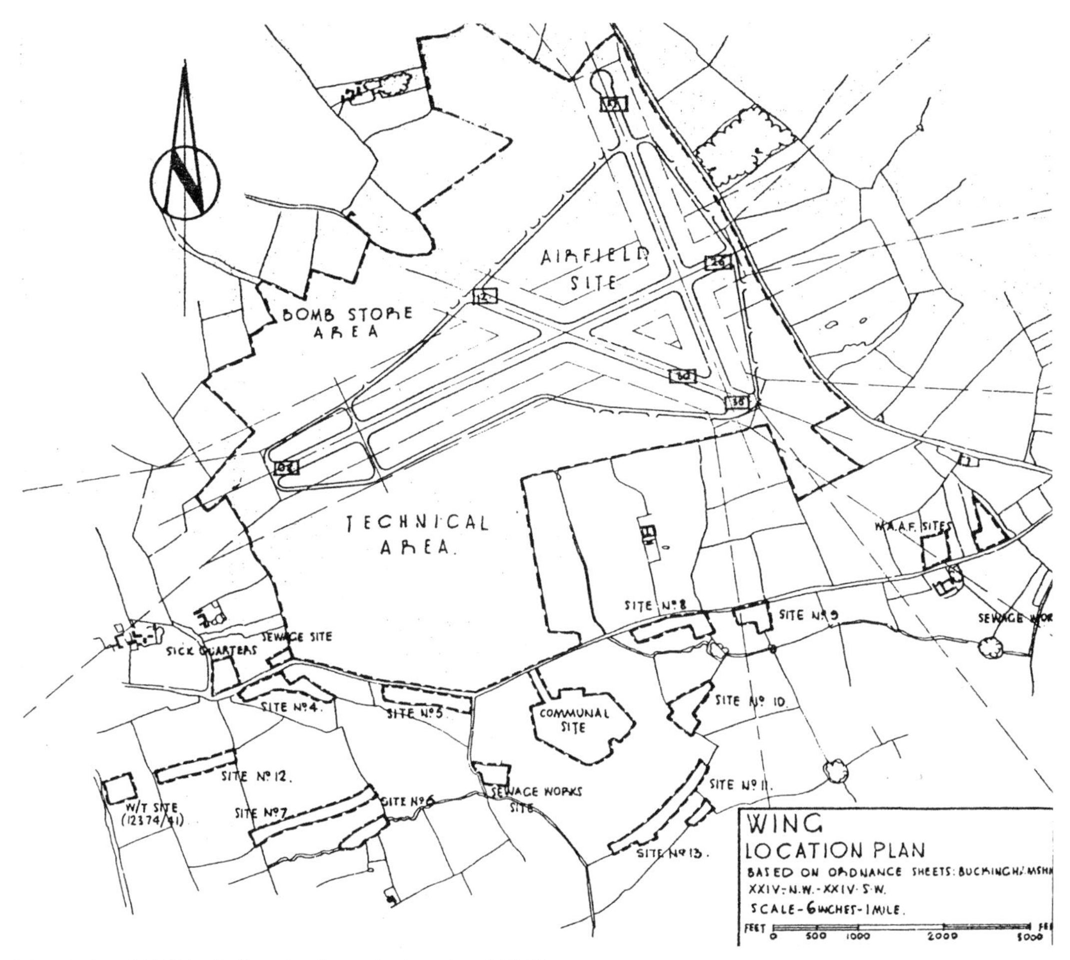

Plan of the airfield including the domestic sites, dated 1945.

been renovated and appear to have an extended lifetime ahead of them as workshops or retail outlets. Many of the remaining buildings can be seen in the photographs included within these pages, and to visit them leaves a poignant feeling, taking the visitor back to those remarkable days when such a peaceful corner of the English countryside bristled with activity.

Fred Capron, a Leading Aircraftman at the station from 1942 - 45 tells the following tale concerning the construction of the airfield,

> 'Before the airfield was operational there was much clearing up by Contractors and Airmen. There was a small orchard still remaining after some of the buildings had been cleared. The Wing Commander arranged for an airman who worked on the land in

peacetime to take a party to dig up the saplings and replant them outside his bungalow. In digging, the lads were a 'little careless' and roots were chopped off and when replanted the trees were supported by stones and rubble. The 'Mad Wingco' as he was known, must have become suspicious by the speed of the transplanting and came out to inspect. 'Will this tree have apples on next year?' he asked. 'Hopefully, yes,sir,' came the reply. Pointing to another tree he asked the same question and received the same reply. Pointing to a third tree he again asked if it would have apples on next year to which he received a reply in the negative. 'And why not?' demanded the Wing Commander. 'Because it's a plum tree, sir,' retorted the airman.'

CHAPTER 2
The Airfield Site

The main runway on the airfield ran roughly WSW to ENE towards the Wing to Stewkley Road, ending just a few metres short of the boundary fence. Ted Sweet remembers,

> 'The main runway had a pronounced dip about two-thirds of the way along its length and at the top of the hump an airman was on duty to wave a red flag informing of the take off of an aircraft. The aircraft would actually disappear from sight in the dip then reappear within a minute before roaring into the air.'

Further memories of the runway come from J.H.Berry,

> 'It had a peculiar slope on the approach side and the Wellington was a bit of a floater so if you were coming in a little bit fast or high, then you missed the first bit of runway and then seemed to be, to a novice, almost in outer space.'

Around the perimeter were 30 dispersal pans for the aircraft to stand on, six almost adjacent to the Stewkley Road fence. An impressive sight the Wellingtons must have been to those travelling along the road. They certainly left an impression on the young John Thornton.

> 'Day and night the Wimpeys went and came. The landing approach for the main runway lay directly above the spinney. Wheels down and flaps down they descended majestically – the changing light of every hour flattering their elegance and poise . Once, a Whitley flew in – gawky and alien in this our field of elegant birds.'

The airmen too were proud of their Wimpeys and John was lovingly shown the secrets of the Wellington by one such flier.

> 'The strength of its geodetic design, the economical use of space, the comfortable layout of the cockpit, the efficiency of the gun turrets. The Wimpey aroma of fabric and 100 octane exhaust must have been one of the most unmistakable and pleasant scents of the war.'

This rather romantic viewpoint may not be entirely shared by all those who flew in the Wellington. Jeffrey Harrington was wary of the ease with which they burnt.

> 'One very dark night we had been driven out to dispersal, climbed aboard and settled down whilst the engines were started up. One engine was started and running, when there was a flash and a bang followed by a billowing cloud of acrid smoke. We evacuated the kite in record time!'

We had to wait some time for the ground crew to cycle out to find us, which they eventually managed by flashing their torches into all the dispersal bays until we were located. It was quite eerie really as we could hear them chatting to each other as they cycled but all we could see

View of the remains of the main runway looking ENE taken from a balloon in 1997. To the left are the bungalows built for the workers at the chicken farm, some of the sheds of which can also be seen. Also clearly visible is Kemsall Wood. (V.H.)

Another view from the balloon showing the hedge running across the centre of the photo which follows the line of the main runway. Also visible are the chicken sheds alongside part of the North/South runway (V.H.)

was the occasional gleam of a cycle lamp or torch. We had no torches or means of communicating with them until they were near. However, all they found wrong was a poor battery connection which had arced under the load of starting the second engine. But you couldn't be too careful, Wimpeys were like tinder boxes.'

Denis Down suggests that aircrew thought quite highly of the reliability of the well worn but faithful Wimpys, but were less happy that they were rather cold.

> 'I can still remember the condensation dripping from my oxygen mask and forming little blobs of ice on my chart.'

Although the various types of Wellington were the main aircraft at Wing, many other types were seen at one time or another, as J.H. Keen's boyhood memories recall.

> 'For several weeks the famous Sharks Mouth squadron of Kittyhawks were at Wing after their duty in the Far East. They had a sharks mouth painted on the radiator – very exciting to us children. I remember that they used to land from a steep dive over the road, very dramatic!'

He also mentions having seen Spitfires, a Blackburn, a Gladiator, a Catalina, a Mosquito and his first helicopter! As stated elsewhere there were numerous other types of aircraft that at one time or another were actually part of 26 OTU, such as the Anson, Martinet, Miles Master, Defiant, Oxford, Hurricane, Tomahawk and Lysander so along with visiting Warwicks, Halifaxes, Lancasters, Stirlings and Liberators, Wing was a veritable paradise for plane spotters, especially if you were a child and not too heavily preoccupied with the traumas of the war!

The Watch Office, now more commonly known as the control tower, was positioned to the south of the main runway in a central position ensuring as good a view of as much of the airfield as possible. It was on two levels with a stairwell, a design that was common to many OTUs.

Five hangars were positioned adjacent to the perimeter track, four of them the T2 design along with a single B1. The former could be erected quickly and measured 121x240ft with a clear door height of 29ft. They were used for aircraft storage and maintenance as was the B1 which was slightly larger.

On the Technical Site were many other buildings associated with an OTU such as the Night Flying Equipment Store, Photographic Block – used for processing pictures taken during reconnaissance, camera gun footage and raid interpretation shots, Parachute Store – a vital role being the checking, packing and issue of these and the Fire Tender Shelter.

All around the airfield could be found blast shelters providing protection, should it have been necessary, for crews at dispersal pans or domestic sites for example.

Also included on the Airfield Site was the Station Office and Operation Block which would have included canteen, rest rooms, Wireless/telegraphy room and telephone exchange.

In the midst of this site stood South Tinkers Hole Farm whose farmhouse and outbuildings were taken over for use as Airmen's Offices and Stores and which reverted to a working farm after the War and remains as such to this day.

Montage of photographs of the first station Monthly Parade 27.11.43 with Hangars 1 and 2 clearly visible. (Copyright Public Records Office Air 26/669).

The perimeter track photographed in 1997 from the same position as the previous photos. Buildings to the right are recent, having replaced the demolished hangar. (author)

The remainder of RAF Wing was made up of numerous other sites. The main entrance was on the Wing to Cublington Road with the Instructional Site the first to be encountered after turning off the road. This would have been where the Ground Training took place. Here were to be found the Instruction rooms, Gunnery Crew and Procedure Centre and the Wireless/Telegraphy(W/T) Operational Instruction Block, along with rest rooms for pilots and crews.

Specialist Training blocks were also to be found, such as that housing the Link Trainer which incorporated a basic representation of an aircraft cockpit with control column and simple instruments. Another was the Turret Trainer which housed a gun turret firing against a projected image. Turret instruction buildings were used to teach escape procedure.

The other areas that made up the airfield included the Defence Site, the Bomb Store Site –

Remains of two buildings forming part of the Wireless/Telegraphy Operational Instruction Block, photographed in March 1997. (author)

The one remaining door in situ in the Wireless/Telegraphy Operational Instruction Block. (author)

positioned to the north of the main runway well away from the other sites – and the Domestic and Communal Sites.

The Communal Site included such features as the Officers' Mess and Sergeants' Mess, the Airmen's Dining Room and various stores. In one complex was to be found the Church and Gymnasium, whilst also on this site could be found the Cinema, tailors, barbers and shoemakers shops. The Commanding Officer's Quarters were also situated on the Communal Site, as was the Post Office.

In addition to the sites mentioned were the WAAF Site and Sick Quarters to be found along the Wing to Cublington road but at opposite ends of the whole site with the latter nearer Cublington, as well as a Sewage disposal site and a Wireless/Telegraphy Site.

John Thornton recalls another group of buildings,

> 'In the home field half a mile NE of the main runway, a direction finding wireless hut was erected with a brick blast proof wall and a huge sheet of copper buried for earthing. A small residential hut lay further NE near the spinney immediately behind the farm buildings of Mount Pleasant.'

Contact with the personnel on the Station was pleasurable as John remembers,

> 'Morris (Roberts) a sheep farmer chummed up with the Clerk of Works of the airfield. Soon the runways were finished and no sooner than the concrete was dry the Wimpeys flew in and they were dispersed on the round concrete pads that surrounded the field. That summer the COW offered all the airfield grass to Morris for hay. They would cut it with a trailer mower and all we had to do was rake, lift and carry it off as soon as we could. Sounded like a real gift when increased ploughing meant that hay grassing was in shorter and shorter supply.'

He continues,

> 'We were friends too with the wireless operators and saw them every day. They liked

the fresh milk and had RAF rations surplus to requirements, which they gave cheerfully to us. They operated mostly at night supporting Wimpeys on night target bombing practice.'

The remains of the Church, the first building on entry to the Communal Site. At the other end of the building was the Gymnasium. (author)

Copy of original envelope postmarked RAF Station Post Office, Wing, dated 7th April 1944. (J.N.)

CHAPTER 3
So This Is Wing!

From January 1944, aircrew personnel, on arrival at this Unit, were given a small booklet entitled, 'So This Is Wing'. It served as a guide book giving information relating to travel directions, entertainment, facilities at the Station and personnel available for assistance with problems of all natures.

It opened with these words,

> 'Welcome to Wing and here's to a happy stay. What's more, here's the 'gen' on how to make the best of it.'

No doubt this friendly introduction to the Station helped ease the newcomers in. Their stay may have been only a couple of months or so, perhaps not long enough to experience all the facilities on offer, but the emphasis was undoubtedly on maintaining morale with much of the booklet stressing the entertainments available. This included the Camp Cinema situated on the Communal Site,

> '....who wants to be always on the highways and byways? We run our OWN cinema... two shows every night except Thursday, films direct from the renters, just like any civvy show, and only a bit behind them for the latest stuff – real 35mm. Times and programmes outside the cinema on your way to the Dining Hall.'

Close up of the lettering on the cinema entrance. (author)

The 'chummy' tone of this part of the booklet continues with details of other entertainment on offer,

> 'ENSA Shows once a fortnight on Thursday (that's why there's no cinema!) and our very own production STUDIO NIGHT – every other fortnight... Don't miss it – it's full of local colour.... Camp Commentary, our own band and individual musical talent, our own jokes and comics. Buckshee shows from time to time.'

And there was more in the form of Station dances, Music Circle and Brains Trust. To find out what was on and when, personnel were urged to look for announcements in the Daily Routine Orders with the following advice,

> 'They are worth reading these DRO's and if you value your happiness, keep well up to date with them and steer clear of trouble. Good tip, that.'

The remains of the entrance to the cinema on the Communal Site, photographed in 1977. (author)

The Music Circle 1944. Education Officer Flt. Lt Hutchinson is seen putting on the record. Making notes is Intelligence Officer Flt. Lt Miller whilst Sgt Coleman studies a record label and F/Sgt Williamson meditates. (I.C.)

As stated earlier the booklet containing such information was available on arrival, but for many, getting to the airfield was in itself fraught with problems. Here, Lewis Shaw, who arrived in Britain from Australia only in January for Gunnery training, describes the difficulties he encountered.

> 'We alighted at Leighton Buzzard Railway Station on 22nd February 1944. It was a cold day and, as usual, transport had not arrived. We trooped into the Waiting Room, which had a fireplace but no fire. We were informed by people waiting for their trains that owing to shortages no fires were being lit. It was noticed that around the walls of the room were fading signs advertising such things as 'Come To The Riviera' and 'Holidays In Nice' etc. We all had the same thoughts and in a few moments some of these plywood signs were taken down and broken up and together with the help of newspapers a fire was lit. We soon had a warm room to the delight of the civilians. Soon after the Station Master came in and was somewhat suspicious at the spectacle. However, seeing a bunch of determined Australians he hastily withdrew to his own office (and fire!). After about an hour and a half, transport finally arrived and we reluctantly set out on that bleak day for Wing, leaving a happy crowd behind.'

Allan Hardwicke was more than likely in that very same group of Gunners, for he too arrived in England in January and like Lewis Shaw, travelled to Wing from Brighton in February. He recalls that the palings of the platform fence were particularly useful in keeping the fire going!

Jeffrey Harrington remembers arriving at Wing in May 1943, before the introduction of the booklet.

> 'We were allocated quarters and each given our 'Arrival Chit' which was a piece of paper on which was printed all the various departments of the Unit. One had to report to each department in the correct order to register arrival, to be given the necessary equipment and advised of times and places of various events important to one's purpose for being there. There were seventeen crews arriving that day, of what was to be Course Number 26, all pursuing the same obstacle course around the camp. Some were going in groups, others singly, causing log jams of bodies in various departments. We got to know our way about and grew to recognise some of our colleagues of other aircrew categories as we bumped into them in the various offices and stores. All of us navigators had come from the same course at Bobbington, so we knew each other well. The first indication we had that Wing was a radically different kind of establishment to any we had previously encountered was revealed by the notice outside the Guardroom which read, 'The fatality record of this Station for last month was ONE FATALITY PER 10 FLYING HOURS'. As we were to fly in Wellingtons for some five or more hours at a time, the arithmetic did not make for feelings of security nor longevity.'

To help make everyone welcome there was the NAAFI as well as the Officers' and Sergeants' Messes. The Corporals had their own Corporals' Club both for RAF and WAAF personnel, including sales counter, reading room and games room (snooker, billiards, table tennis and the intriguingly named snookerette). The YMCA was open to all ranks whilst the WAAFs had their

Sgt. Joe Coleman from the Photographic/Intelligence Section pointing out the intricacies of the V1 in the News Room at Wing – June 1944. (I.C.)

More studious personnel in the News Room. (I.C.)

own NAAFI on their site. A News Room, Quiet Room and Library were also available. Further details of the various ways in which personnel relaxed are to be found in a later chapter.

As well as acting as a general guide, the booklet also made it perfectly clear what was expected of aircrew at the Unit under the heading,

'A Word Of Advice To Aircrew Personnel – What Wing expects of you.'

The best way to appreciate this is to reproduce the exact words from the booklet.

'We're out for a very high standard. By far the greater number of you arrive here with newly acquired rank, commissioned or non commissioned and expect rightly the privileges which rank confers. BUT rank brings RESPONSIBILITIES and the privileges are there to enable you to fulfil these responsibilities. Have you ever given thought to the feelings of the old time Senior NCO, Warrant Officer or Commissioned Officer who has worked long years to get what you have got in a matter of months? How much more critical would they be if you go about 'dropping bricks' all over the place. Had they EVER been seen minus hat, hands in pockets, buttons undone, lax in saluting, in a smart, self-satisfied way, they would NEVER have got their stripes, their warrant or their commission. What does it all boil down to? Just this, that you have a lot to catch up on. Learn good mess manners. Be smart in appearance and habits. Pay your superiors the respect and compliments due to them. You cannot get just that discipline which saves lives in a tight corner in the air without that extra something which makes you a shining example to others.'

Unfortunately, the author of these stirring words is not named, although it sounds as if it ought to be the Commanding Officer. Whoever penned them certainly did so from the heart, and it would come as no surprise to learn that they made the required impact upon many a young and impressionable airman. What is interesting is the complete change of tone from the earlier sections of the booklet that are more 'friendly'; however it cannot be said that the airmen were not put in the picture as to how they were expected to conduct themselves.

At least they had the Christmas entertainment to look forward to. This took the form of a special Studio Night, which in 1943 had the title, 'From The Sublime' and was enhanced by a variety of dances, films and activities, as follows:

20.12.43 – Fancy Dress In Airmen's NAAFI
21.12.43 – Officers' Mess Dance
22.12.43 – Cinema – 'Crash Dive'
23.12.43 – Cinema – as above
24.12.43 – Cinema – as above
25.12.43 – Treasure Hunt – Football,Hockey and Rugby matches. Old Fashioned Music Hall including Talent Competition Cinema – as above.
26.12.43 – Boxing Day Dance – Airmen's NAAFI
27.12.43 – Cinema – as above
30.12.43 – ENSA Concert
31.12.43 – New Year's Eve Ball – Sergeants' Mess

Such was life at the Unit, with most important of all, the reason for its existence, the long hours of training and the work on aircraft, which continued through to closure in 1946.

CHAPTER 4
The Training of Aircrew

The main role of the airfield was of course to prepare crews for flying. This was dependent on good quality instructors and aircraft that were well maintained.

Following basic RAF training, those accepted for aircrew moved from their ITW to an EFTS, whilst those accepted for ground crew went to a technical training establishment.

At the EFTS they received their first taste of flying and its hazards, including flight-sickness. Often initial flying was learnt in Tiger Moths or Oxfords, with instructors being older pilots rested from operational flying.

After a period of some ten weeks and possibly a spell at an SFTS the would-be pilots were sent to the OTUs to fly the type, or similar type of aircraft they would use in an operational squadron. At Wing this proved to be the Vickers Wellington bomber, affectionately known as the Wimpy after the character in the Popeye cartoons J. Wellington Wimpy.

In the 92 Group Training Syllabus the aim of the OTU is clearly stated,

> 'To produce aircrews commanded by Captains capable of carrying out bombing operations against the enemy in Wellington aircraft. It is therefore the final stage of training.'

Each OTU was linked to the respective Bomber, Fighter or Coastal Commands and after completion of this stage of training aircrew would then move on to a squadron or in the case of some Bomber crews, a Conversion Unit, to become familiar with flying four engined aircraft rather than the twin-engined Wellingtons at the OTU. The time spent at each stage of training was regularly revised to ensure enough crews were available to join squadrons especially after heavy losses in May 1940.

The intake at OTUs was initially 45 pilots every two weeks from April 1941 along with 40 wireless operators/air gunners and 20 each of air gunners and observers. This however, varied from Course to Course, and by 1944 the numbers at Wing were more likely to be around 16 of each with a large number of personnel being from Australia, Canada and New Zealand. A pilot was expected to have flown some 260 hours before arriving at an OTU, but this again would be reduced in subsequent years.

Each of the crew members would receive training from Screened Instructors. These were aircrew who had already completed a tour of operations and were now 'resting', as John Whitworth DFC confirms.

> 'I was at Wing from early March 1943 until September 1944 as a screened pilot/instructor. I arrived as a Sergeant back from the North African desert having

Pilots of Number 5 course photographed 25.6.42. P/O Harris, Sgt Downs, Sgt Carson, Sgt Kidd, Sgt Ogilvie, Sgt Streeter and Sgt Looney were all involved in the Thousand Bomber Raids during September 1942. The last two mentioned lost their lives in these less than three months after this photograph was taken. See the chapter entitled '26 OTU In Action' for details. (I.C.)

completed a 37 ops tour (250 hours) with 37 Squadron.'

The Training Syllabus makes the following points about the role of the instructor.

'The quality of the instruction depends entirely upon the quality of the instructors. All instructors must – know their job thoroughly, be capable of describing and demonstrating clearly and go at a rate at which the trainee can absorb the training.'

Pilots arrived from their SFTS having flown most likely in Oxfords without a crew and one of the first tasks was to "crew up" with a Navigator, Observer/Bomb Aimer, Wireless Operator/Air Gunner and Rear Gunner. This was later to change to a six man crew including the pilot and navigator along with an Air Bomber/Bomb Aimer, Wireless Operator/Air Gunner and two further air gunners for the rear and mid-upper turrets.

As Ken Annable, who was at RAF Wing for the year July 1943-44, as an instructor, comments,

'We allowed them a certain amount of choice as to which crew they joined.'

A further insight into the crewing-up procedure comes from Ted Sweet,

'..in the same office block 16 pilots were reporting to the Chief Flying Officer, 16 navigators to the Navigation Leader and 16 bomb aimers to the Bombing Leader. 32 air gunners were reporting to the Gunnery Leader. All had arrived from AFUs to be welded together into 16 bomber crews. The next day Squadron Leader Gorrie told the aircrews who had gathered to form themselves into crews by 1700 hours. After this time there was to be no changing. Each pilot would select two air gunners who must then decide themselves who would be rear gunner. Often crew paired themselves with others from earlier training schools, but eventually crews came together.'

Cliff Stewart arrived at Wing as a newly promoted Sergeant air gunner in June 1943 and remembers the day he was crewed up,

'Until they reached the OTU, all aircrews were trained separately, air gunners at one unit, pilots at another and so on. Naturally when it came to being made up into crews everyone wanted the best pilot, the best navigator etc as our lives depended on each other. We were all led to a hangar and told to sort ourselves out. Fortunately I was already on good terms with another gunner. He wanted to be a mid-upper gunner and I wanted to be the tail gunner. This is supposed to be the most dangerous place on the aircraft but I thought I would rather depend on my own shooting, much as I had reasonable confidence in my 'oppo'. After a couple of hours we were crewed up'.

Jack Lunn, at Wing in July 1943,having completed pilot training at Cranwell recalls his crewing up, confirming its rather pot-luck arrangement.

'I stood talking to my pilot friend Doug Ford when the Navigator he had chosen asked if I had a Navigator. I hadn't, so he introduced me to Al Trennery and we decided to make a go of it together. Then I spoke to another bloke and he was a farmer's boy (like me), so he was in. Another bloke approached us by the name of Lister and we interrogated him before he was in. We were then approached by a rear gunner left over from previous courses and finally a Canadian bomb aimer.'

Harry McLean tells an amusing tale of how he was crewed up with a Wing Commander.

Number 6 Course pilots. Sgt Flack, Sgt Lowe, Sgt Welford, Sgt Easter, Sgt Rogers and Sgt Hage were involved in the Thousand Bomber Raids. The last named did not return. (I.C.)

Pilots, Air Gunners, Navigators, Navigators and Wireless Operators from Number 10 Course. (I.C.)

'Thinking a Pilot Officer must be better than a Sergeant I asked one if he had himself a gunner. He replied that he had. The next day when I saw the chap again he asked me if I had got myself fixed up. I was about to reply in the negative when I had a sudden flash of humour. I told him that I was flying with the Wing Commander. He looked incredulous and asked 'Really?' and I replied 'Oh yes, I asked him and he said he would be glad to have me'. I thought no more of this until the next morning, when I was told the Wing Commander wished to see me. My God, I thought, you've done it now! When I reported to the Wing Commander, it was exactly as I had joked. He said, 'I hear you're looking for a pilot?' I replied that I was and he then said 'If I'll do for you then you will do for me."

This procedure is well remembered by all but was considered a successful method despite its haphazard appearance, as Bruce Giles states.

'It was a smart move by the RAF with the whole thing being carried out for them rather than by them. It was also good psychology because the matching process did work very well.'

Bruce was a pilot from Australia and soon began looking for his crew; it was May 1944.

'Firstly I cornered two RAF gunners who were obviously sticking together. Yes they would take me if they could stay together – OK by me. Next, looking round I spotted a wireless operator in RAAF dark blue battle dress with whom I had been acquainted at school in Australia – quite amazing. He apparently took the view – the better the devil you know. Next, up popped a very likely looking navigator, RAF, a serious responsible looking type and after looking me up and down he said 'yes'. Almost immediately an unattached bomb aimer looking a mature, dignified bloke came under my spell: I would never believe I had the cheek!'

And there was another crew formed

Bruce Giles – Pilot
Bernard Cooper – Navigator
Reg Bonner – Air Bomber
Ted Henry – Wireless Operator
Alan Chettoe – Rear Gunner
Hal Bosworth – Mid Upper Gunner

J.H. Berry was another pilot seeking out a crew in July 1943,

'I was sitting with a navigator whom I had a good feeling about and after a while I decided to make a go of it. He said that we ought to get cracking or else we'd be left with the odds and sods. This we did and very soon we had a wireless operator and two gunners leaving us only a bomb aimer to co-opt. This wasn't so easy as they were all Canadian and my navigator wasn't best pleased at the thought! But get one we did.'

It was customary that, once united, crew members moved on to Squadrons together with the close relationships forged at the various training establishments cementing a special bond between them. Relationships that still exist to this day. As J.H.Berry remarks about the above crew,

Further trainees from Number 10 Course. According to Harry McLean, P/O Etienne was the only black trainee at 26 OTU. He was killed on 5.3.43 when his aircraft crashed into the sea during a raid on Essen whilst with 214 Squadron. (I.C.)

Pilots from Number 10 Course including Wing Commander Earle. (I.C.)

'This mish-mash all survived the War.'

Harry McLean continued flying with Wing Commander Earle at Dalton in Yorkshire where the latter became First Commanding Officer of 428 RCAF Bomber Squadron and was eventually to retire as Air Chief Marshal Sir Alfred "Tubby" Earle CBE,CB,KBE,GBE.

In some cases the coming together of crew members began before the day allotted. Harry George, Bomb Aimer/Observer, came to Wing in September 1943.

> 'I arrived at Leighton Buzzard station and went to a cafe which was at the bottom of the road leading to Wing. I was enjoying a cup of tea when in walked a Sergeant in a RAAF greatcoat. I asked where he was off to and found that he too was going to Wing. Further conversation followed and I discovered that he was a Navigator who had recently finished training in Canada. His name was Chigwidden, (Chick, as he was better known). By aircrew standards he was quite old as he must have been all of thirty years of age. We were preparing to make our way to Wing when in walked another chap and in my impetuous, youthful way I pulled aside his greatcoat top to reveal the coveted Wings. 'We have a crew!' I remarked.'

Harry also recalls going to the hangar to complete the crewing up procedure where, indeed, the rest of the crew were assembled.

Jeffrey Harrington remembers that,

> 'Once crewed up each crew was given a number, which together with the Course number and surname of the individual, was worn on a leather strip on the right breast of the battle dress blouse.'

Having formed a crew it was down to the business of training.

Every aspect of this was clearly set out in the Training Syllabus and the full programme lasted a mere ten weeks. The amount crammed in to that short time is quite staggering.

I do not intend to reproduce the Training Syllabus here, but will endeavour to give a flavour of what was necessary in order to complete the course.

There were two periods of Air Training both consisting of 40 hours of flying – Basic Flying Training and Applied Flying Training. Alongside this came three periods of Ground Training.

The whole process began with two weeks Initial Ground Training which was undertaken at Wing rather than Little Horwood. No flying was undertaken during this part of the Syllabus. Each crew member had instruction relevant to their own area as well as that necessary for the entire crew.

For example, Discipline was the first part of the Ground Training with those aspects relevant to Captaincy highlighting the control. Airmanship covered numerous aspects, including amongst others, 'the acquiring of air sense', airfield discipline, exercises using the Instructional Fuselages, procedures for night flying, ditching and rescue, cockpit drill and knowledge of the aircraft and its performance. Some of the lectures under this heading were for pilots only but many involved all crew members.

Training in Medical aspects was given including that relating to hygiene and Venereal Disease. There were lectures on photography and meteorology plus a great emphasis on physical fitness, for as the manual states,

> 'It is an accepted fact that modern operational flying conditions necessitate a very high standard of physical fitness to equip crews for the conditions of mental and physical strain likely to be encountered.'

A minimum of three hours per week of physical training was therefore included for all crew members plus involvement in organised sports on one half day. Lectures in Navigation included the use of the sextant and the Astro Compass, Star Recognition, Gee manipulation and Map Reading, amongst many others.

Gunners were made conversant with Warning and Fighting Manoeuvres, firing and turret manipulation, sighting, aircraft recognition and range estimation amongst numerous other aspects all crammed into the fortnight.

Training for bombing was summed up in an introductory paragraph in the training manual as follows and is worth dwelling upon, for, of course, this was the reason for the Unit's existence.

> 'The aim of the bombing syllabus is to produce a crew which can operate efficiently as a bombing team. This team consists of Pilot, Air Bomber, and Navigator, and each must appreciate his responsibility for accurate bombing, and be capable of carrying out efficiently the duties entailed. All instruction and analysis of exercises must, therefore, aim at encouraging crew co-operation.'

It is also interesting to look at the duties of each member of this team as outlined in the Training Syllabus.

The Air Bomber was to take responsibility for the direction of the aircraft during the run up and attack, and for the accurate aiming of the bombs. He was regarded as the key man in the team and the authority on bombs and bombing.

The Pilot's main duty was deemed to be the accurate flying of the aircraft whilst his appreciation of the requirements of accurate bombing and the extent of his co-operation with the Air Bomber were vital with regards to the accuracy of the bombing.

The role of the Navigator during bombing raids was to be responsible for wind finding and computing the data required for the bombsight, and for the initial stage of the bombing run. He was also expected to be able to release the bombs in an emergency.

Other crew members were given instruction to enable them to understand the problems involved in a bombing attack and handle pyrotechnics.

Thus, the training for bombing over the entire ten weeks was to prime all crew members to be in a position to undertake bombing raids with the utmost confidence and efficiency.

The Wireless Operators were given 48 hours of lectures in all aspects of their role whilst all crew received some training in Signals and Communication. The final part of the Initial Ground Training came under the heading of Intelligence. This covered such aspects as Security, including "careless talk", Geography, knowledge of Bomber Command Offensive and German Defences such as Night Fighter systems, Flak Defences and searchlights.

As can be seen from the details given, this early part of the syllabus was very comprehensive.

Bomb Aimers from Number 4 Course photographed in 1942. (I.C.)

Bomb Aimers from Number 5 Course – June 1942. (I.C.)

The Lectures lasted one hour and were given by specialist officers many of whom travelled around the OTUs although each Unit had its own officers specialising in certain departments. Intelligence Officers, for example, would lecture on such subjects as target identification, using aerial photographs, or the recognition of aircraft, using the shapes and silhouettes of models. Those delivering the lectures received this instruction in the Training Syllabus manual.

> 'Long lectures during which the Instructor is wondering how he is going to fill the time allotted to him are particularly to be avoided.'

As well as a mass of additional aspects, many of those covered during this initial fortnight were expanded upon during the remaining two periods of Ground Training.The next of these ran alongside the Basic Flying Training which took place at Little Horwood for a four week period. It was therefore necessary for crew members to move to the satellite airfield, all that is except the Navigators who remained at Wing for a further ten days during which time they flew as Second Navigators and continued with their basic training.

Ron Stotter has a distinct memory on arriving for his navigator training.

> 'We were taken to the Navigation Hut for an introductory talk and to meet the Chief Navigation Officer. On entering the hut I couldn't help but notice the sign over the door, which read,
>
> SEMPER – IN – EXCRETA
>
> We now knew what to expect!'

Jeffrey Harrington recalls part of his navigator training,

> 'We navigators who remained at Wing did more tutorials and a number of hairy, simulated flights in a 'mock up' in which the clock was set to run at twice the normal speed. The flights were made to seem more realistic by placing us in small cubicles where we were bombarded with engine sound and had to work like the clappers to keep up with the demonic racing clock. After a couple of weeks of general and emergency procedure training, the navigators were at last initiated into the wonders of 'Gee' – the magic box of tricks that enabled us to pinpoint ourselves with a degree of accuracy determined by our proximity to the transmitting chain and our ability to correctly interpolate the blips on the screen. It did require a degree of skill to operate and assess the readings accurately and was subject to jamming, but so far as we were concerned it was for navigation what the rubber tyre was for motoring! Everything about 'Gee' was cloaked in secrecy. If we were obliged to land on an airfield other than one of Bomber Command, the aircraft had to have an armed guard and the charts had to be destroyed.'

Ron Stotter has similar memories of the Gee.

> 'We were assured that this new equipment would enable us to be accurate in our navigation to within a couple of hundred yards – a massive improvement on Astro navigation.
>
> The technology and the hardware were so secret and well guarded that we were taken

More pilots from Number 10 Course pictured with some from Number 8 course – September 1942. (I.C.)

under armed guard to the room in which the equipment was installed. The door was locked and the guards would remain at their post outside the room. Many hours were spent under theoretical and practical instruction. The more we learned about it and used it the greater became our admiration and respect for this wonder navigation aid. We were convinced that never again would we get lost. It was only later that we were to learn that it had a limited range beyond the UK and also that should the equipment be out of service, that would be no reason to cancel an operation. In those circumstances we would have to revert to the basic navigation we were taught when working to gain our Wings.'

John Boxall also received navigator training at 26 OTU and he too has a story to tell concerning the remarkable Gee.

'The poor old navigator was always laden down when going to the aircraft, his navigation bag full of maps, charts, air almanac tables, together with his sextant, parachute, etc, so that when on local flying one normally left the bulk of this behind. One night we were up on local flying and I only had my parachute and the Gee chart of the local area. If one needed to return to base it was only necessary to set the Gee co-ordinates on the 'box' and perform a Gee homing. On this particular night fog started to drift in and all the aircraft were recalled, (as long as visibility was around 600 yards one could do a visual landing). After the third attempt at landing we were informed by the watch tower that if we did not land on the next attempt we were to divert to RAF Honeyborne. This aerodrome was not in the area covered by the local Gee chart and as I had no other navigation equipment with me this would have meant asking for the Gee co-ordinates for Honeyborne or requesting radio bearings or courses to steer, and I would have been in trouble with the Navigation leader at Wing on return. Fortunately we were able to land at the fourth attempt and I learnt my lesson and never flew again without full equipment on all future flights even if they were ten minute air tests.'

The Basic Flying Training that was undertaken at Little Horwood consisted of all flying training of an individual nature and also that which, in its early stages, involved co-operation between two members of the crew. Conversion to flying Wellingtons, Bombing and Gunnery training were all covered at this stage.

Don Abercrombie was a bomb aimer who remembers,

'On 16th July 1944 we began our familiarisation of the mighty Wimpy. This was mainly for the pilots who were being introduced for the first time to an aircraft in the 1000 hp range and these initially brief excursions into the heavens gave the rest of the crew the opportunity to assess the prowess of our captain – 'Rog' – Eric Rogers who was an 'old codger' of 32, the rest of us averaging 19. He passed all phases with flying colours and our confidence was established.'

Two identical 'flights' were involved, given the titles A and B Flights, with intakes being received by each Flight alternately every two weeks. During this period, a third Flight – E –

assisted by providing certain gunnery training facilities. Trainees were passed with their aircraft from A and B flights to E flight on a daily basis.

The flying consisted of dual day flying, that is pilot and instructor (screened pilot), followed by solo day flying and then a similar arrangement at night. A total of forty hours flying was experienced by the pilot with training in circuits and landings, one engine flying and overshoot procedures.

J.H.Berry recalls the Night Flying exercises, suggesting that,

> 'Today, I would doubt if anyone would be able to experience the darkness of those nights. There was no light and no reflected glow from towns or cities. It was black.'

Bombing training at this stage included both day and night flying and crews were required to pass test exercises over the bombing ranges. On return to the airfield each member of the bombing team was required to attend discussions analysing their results.

As for the Gunners their training included firing at a drogue being towed as fast as possible.

Jeffrey Harrington recalls an incident during one such exercise.

> 'We flew out over the North Sea for air firing at cotton target drogues deployed behind the aircraft and the gunners expended all our ammunition, some twenty eight thousand rounds I believe. The racket and smoke that swept through the aircraft was incredible. After he had fired his quota, our wireless operator/air gunner determined to obtain a radio bearing from a ground station. The response he received caused considerable consternation for it came in loud and clear, louder and clearer than it should, and the direction given was obviously wrong. It was a German operator! We slunk home fast and low, with no ammunition with which to defend ourselves and with the German operator knowing our bearing, that bit of the North Sea was no place to be just then.'

Simulation combat with the use of cine-camera guns was another part of the training with the Gunner having to provide a running commentary of the exercise to go with the cine film.

The final part of the whole training programme was called Applied Flying Training and involved all the crew in every flight, under the command of the Captain. It covered day and night cross country flights, with bombing exercises in which the Pilot, Air Bomber and Navigator worked under conditions as near operational as possible and fighter affiliation exercises.

Jeffrey Harrington recalls these,

> 'Fighter affiliation exercises involved being pursued by a number of friendly fighter aircraft who attempted to secure a 'kill' with their cameras. Our gunners also used cameras and the pilot would, amongst other things, execute the dreaded, stomach wrenching, corkscrew manoeuvre in an effort to frustrate the attackers.'

Ken Annable also remembers the Fighter Affiliation exercise.

> 'Fighters based with us would make mock attacks on the aircraft and we would teach the pilots and gunners evasive action. Both the fighter and the rear gunner had camera guns so that tactics and hits could be assessed afterwards.'

The culmination of the training programme was involvement in Bullseye exercises, Air Sea Rescue exercises, Nickel or Feint operations or even actual bombing operations.

Ground School Navigation Staff at RAF Little Horwood, October 1945.
Left to Right: Freddy Reeve, Ray Wickens, Jack Warwick, Norman Relf, Vic Freeman, Freddy Whitmarsh. (J.W.)

The Bullseye is remembered by J.H.Berry as,

'The 'passing out piece'- a night 'raid' to a given target where there would be an infra red marker (invisible to us) which would show a trace on our camera. One could really analyse the bombing run to check how straight and level you had flown the aircraft. Often the local searchlight crews would be alerted to give them practice to see if they could catch us in their beams. This could be quite nasty.'

This final part of the programme took place at Wing as well as the final part of the Ground Training,with trainees joining C and D flights from A and B flights for the four weeks and forty hours flying.

Memories of the various aspects of training are readily recalled by those who experienced them, be they trainees or instructors. Johnny Silvester was a pilot at Wing from August 1942 until January the following year who for much of that time, was attached to E Flight which had been formed to work with the gunnery school, training rear gunners.

'At first we were equipped with Martinets with which we would attack the Wellingtons and they in turn would fire with the cine-camera guns which we could analyse after landing. Later we had infra-red fitted to our wing tips so that the exercise could be carried out at night. The Martinet could also stream a drogue which was operated from the rear position so that live ammo could be used.'

John Whitworth DFC also remembers towing a drogue using a Lysander, an aircraft which he describes as,

'great fun to fly, after a Wimpy. I was lucky to get a lot of hours in on this plane.'

Bob Soutar who was a Pilot Instructor with 26 OTU after returning from ops in the Middle East, also recalls the Lysander.

'It had short landing and take-off capabilities and was equipped with an all moveable tail plane. The trim was therefore wound right back for landing and right forward for take-off, hence its capabilities. I soon learnt that, as on one occasion I took off with the trim wound back and was startled to find myself climbing very rapidly and sweating to get the trim forward. The aircraft was Lysander T1424.'

Of the Martinet, Johnny Silvester remarks,

'It was hardly a fair comparison to the German fighter so we were eventually equipped with Hurricane IIc's that had all their armament stripped out and made an ideal fast fighter for gunnery training. They were a beautiful aircraft to fly and could react to any aerobatic manoeuvre.'

Ken Annable gives further details of some other aspects of the training programme,

'The flying consisted of getting the pilots off solo, so that they were at least safe with their crew, teaching all the characteristics and emergency procedures of the aircraft. All crews did a certain amount of flying plus ground lectures on airmanship, procedures, navigation, meteorology, bombing etc.'

Flying times during training could last anything from 15 minutes to cross-country flights of up to 6 hours. For example, in the Log Book of Len Land, a Sergeant wireless operator at

Wing during 1944, is reference to the following night cross-country flight.

Base (Wing) – Northampton – Reading – 5416N,0227E – Flamboro Head – Flamboro Bombing Range – Doncaster – Fenton Bombing Range – Northampton – Base. Total Flying time 4hrs 40mins.

A further insight into training is given by Cliff Stewart.

> 'We flew to a bombing range on the east coast for bombing practice but air firing took place over the local countryside. Each gunner would fire off about 1000 rounds and I was always amazed that we never heard of anyone being hurt. All we were told to do was always aim at the drogue from below, but the bullets had to land somewhere.'

Desmond Truss, air gunner at Wing during August to October 1944 recalls,

> 'My parents' home was at Summertown, Oxford and as we used to do our high level bombing practice at Otmoor, I persuaded my pilot on a couple of occasions to fly over Southdale Road.'

Harry McLean remembers that,

> 'Gunners did quite a lot of work on stripping guns, mainly the 303 Browning. We also had plenty of clay pigeon shooting, both free standing and with turret mounted shotguns.'

Harry also recalls training in a Decompression chamber in order to get used to working in an oxygen mask and become familiar with the effect of having no oxygen available. This area of training is also recalled by John Boxall who completed his OTU Navigator course at Wing during 1945.

> 'The five crew members would go together with the exercise being under the control of medical staff outside. To illustrate the effects of a lack of oxygen, we were asked to do simple writing tasks and sums and we each had to remove our oxygen masks in turn, with a crew member standing by to replace the mask. Most personnel quickly lost consciousness and when the oxygen mask was replaced they were amazed to see how the writing had tailed off as they passed out.'

Other aspects of training required the use of a practice fuselage, two of which were provided by the stripping down of older Wellingtons in March of 1942. Crewmen practised scrambling through these in full gear before jumping out through the rear doors, sometimes into a strategically placed dinghy.

This practice for abandoning an aircraft continued by having a fuselage fixed higher, requiring the crew to escape through hatches.

This was further extended to provide training to help crews tackle the problem of crash landing on water, as Ted Sweet recalls,

> 'We went to Cambridge Swimming Pool where we had to jump
> off the diving board with blacked-out goggles into the water and then turn a dinghy into position and help each other in.'

One of the early references in the ORB to particular training is the construction of a 'Gropes' room, 'Gropes' being the name given to a form of training that involved flight

An example of the end product of the hectic training schedule – a crew! Standing F/Sgt Tony Lack – Navigator and P/O Peter Sherrard – Bomb Aimer. Seated: F/Lt Colin Steele – Pilot, F/O Jack Robinson – Signaller, Sgt Arthur Hurst – Air Gunner (J.R.).

The same crew as previous page, having returned from a five hour cross-country flight in a Wellington X during 1945. (J.R.)

simulation during which a route had to be planned to reach a particular target on a map. The wireless operator would receive messages to assist and there would even be slides and fake winds created to add to the reality of the exercise.

Such exercises were undoubtably crucial in the aspect of what might be termed as 'teambuilding'.

Ted Sweet refers to a motto found over the Navigation Section at Wing which read,

'MAN IS NOT LOST'

underneath which some wag had written,

> 'But occasionally is completely unaware of his exact location.'

Wireless Operator Keith McLean, an Australian from Minyip, Victoria, was at 26 OTU from October 1944 until February 1945. Having completed his initial training in Canada, Keith recalls an incident dated in his flying log~on 25th November 1944.

> 'On the crew's first solo flight we were told to follow the railway lines, turn and come back. But we hit cloud and when we turned we couldn't see anything, so we climbed above the cloud. Unfortunately we were flying directly towards a number of glider-pulling Stirlings! By the time we had avoided them we were lost but we eventually landed at Hunsdon. After a marvellous meal we were given a good telling off for landing without permission as we had been unable to make radio contact.'

Another incident was recalled on 8th January 1945 when the crew again hit trouble.

> 'We were on a Cross-Country exercise and returned to Little Horwood only to find blizzard conditions making it impossible to land so we were diverted to Colerne not far from Bath where we landed comfortably. We had to stay there for two days but it was rather uncomfortable as we had only our flying kit.'

The crew on both these flights stayed together to move on to 1662 Heavy Conversion Unit at Blyton and from there to 460 Squadron at Binbrook. Another tale from their months at Wing can be found in the Chapter on Operational Flying. They were all Australian

Saxe Coverdale – Captain – Tasmania.
Porrie Lane – Navigator – Perth.
Len Duncan – Bomb Aimer – Sidney.
Johnny Thomas – Air Gunner – Perth.
George Crute – Air Gunner – Donnybrook.
Keith McLean – Wireless Operator – Minyip.

High level practice bombing came towards the latter stages of the training programme with several bombing ranges used including one in the Wash and another off the coast of Essex. Keith McLean remembers one of these exercises with a smile,

> 'The bad weather meant that we had to return to base with our bombs intact – but one actually fell off. We scarpered but thankfully it didn't cause any problems.'

Ted Sweet sums up the training at Wing in a complimentary manner.

> '26 OTU was like a well-oiled machine dedicated to passing on to trainee crews as much

info as they could absorb. No time was wasted and the Wellingtons spent all fine days and nights in the air on training flights. Even on weather doubtful days the Wellingtons were airborne whenever possible. On bad weather days we were kept busy with a full programme of learning throughout the day from one lecture room to another.'

Providing the weather conditions did not delay events, the training lasted 10 weeks and after completion, crews would be ready to join a Wellington operational squadron, although as these became fewer with the advent of Lancasters, Halifaxes and Stirlings they would leave the OTU to go to an HCU for further training with four engined aircraft before then joining an appropriate squadron.

It should never be forgotten that these young men were now qualified as fully trained aircrew and yet were still barely into their twenties, a point emphasised by Harry McLean when he states,

> 'Within five months of joining the RAF I was a fully qualified Sergeant Air Gunner, expected to bomb Germany. The realisation was a bit of a shock.'

Unfortunately, training did not always proceed smoothly and the history of 26 OTU along with all other training units, is littered with accidents, many of which proved fatal for members of the crews.

The following Chapter gives details of some of the tragic accidents related to 26 OTU.

A superb shot from the Wellington flown by F/Lt colin Steele coming in to land at RAF Wing with the runway, perimeter track and hangars clearly visible. This and the previous photo were taken with a pre-war Kodak box camera still in Tony Lack's possession! This photo was taken from the aircraft's astro-dome and shows the fairing for the D/F loop aerial on the left. (T.L.)

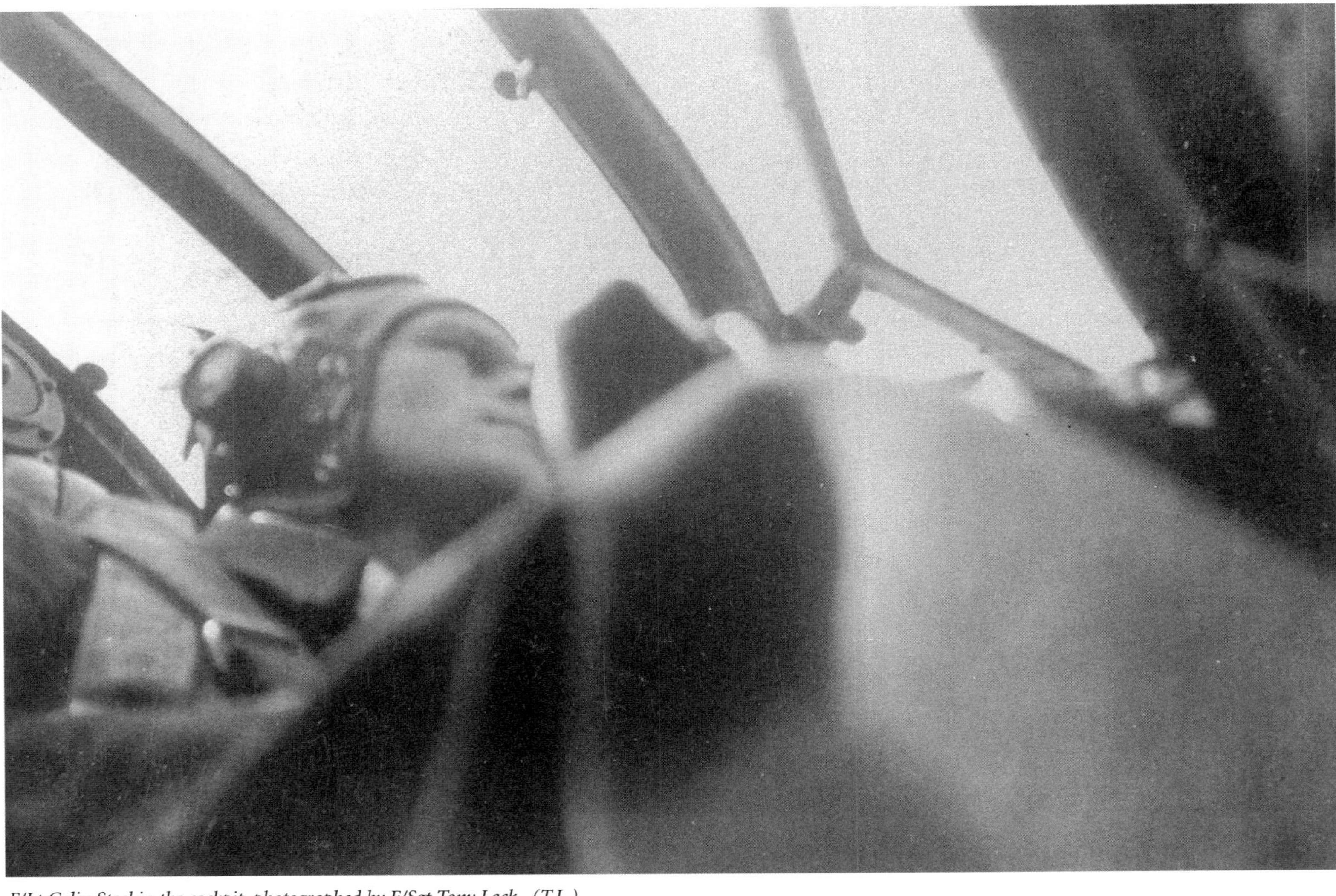

F/Lt Colin Steel in the cockpit, photographed by F/Sgt Tony Lack. (T.L.)

NO 26 O.T.U. WING

Date	Hour	Aircraft Type and No.	Pilot	Duty	Remarks (including results of bombing, gunnery, exercises, etc.)	Flying Times Day	Flying Times Night
					Time carried forward :—	106·20	12·45
1944 MARCH 22	1310	WELLINGTON X 498	P/O BOWELL	WIRELESS OPERATOR	BASE - NORTHAMPTON - GOOLE - PETERBOROUGH - NEWBURY - CHURCH HONEY - NORTHAMPTON - BASE	2·55	
22	1605	498	P/O BOWELL	"	CIRCUITS AND LANDINGS.	1·00	
23	1315	498	P/O HARRINGTON	"	BASE - NORTHAMPTON - GOOLE - PETERBOROUGH - NEWBURY - CHURCH HONEY - NORTHAMPTON - BASE.	3·40	
24	1040	355	P/O HARRINGTON	"	BASE - FISHGUARD - ST. TUDWALS - LANDED AT VALLEY.	2·30	
24	1540	355	P/O HARRINGTON	"	RETURN FROM VALLEY.	1·30	
25	1345	256	P/O HARRINGTON, F/SGT. HARDING	"	FIGHTER AFFILIATION.	·55	
25	1440	256	P/O HARRINGTON	"	FIGHTER AFFILIATION AND HIGH LEVEL BOMBING	2·10	
25	2030	355	P/O WILKINS	"	CIRCUITS AND LANDINGS		·50
27	2020	519	P/O HARRINGTON	"	HIGH LEVEL BOMBING - LANDED AT CRANFIELD		1·50
[illegible]	2010	638	P/O HARRINGTON	"	HIGH LEVEL BOMBING - RETURNED TO BASE		·10
30	1325	638	P/O HARRINGTON	"	BASE - NORTHAMPTON - FISHGUARD - ST. TUDWALS - LINCOLN - BISHOPS STORTFORD - NORTHAMPTON - BASE	4·30	
					TOTAL TIME ...	125·30	15·35

Example page from a typical Flying Log, this belonging to Hugh Richards, a Wireless Operator/Air Gunner at 26 OTU in the spring of 1944. (H.R.)

CHAPTER 5
Accidents

Some of the most vivid memories of personnel at RAF Wing and no doubt at the many other OTUs throughout the country relate, sadly, to accidents in which life was lost.

Accidents during training were commonplace and accepted, it would appear, as inevitable. Despite their enthusiasm and thorough and varied training, the youthful pilots and crew members lacked the experience to help cope with real situations and crises.

News of accidents spread quickly, with aircrew who lost friends or colleagues probably most affected of those at the Unit. Although they might have suggested outwardly that they were philosophical and light-hearted,inwardly they may well have admitted to suffering from that awful, 'it could be me next', feeling.

How the Unit in general reacted to such disasters related to some extent to the examples set by senior officers, suggests Sam Lawton.

> 'Anything negative, or which might cause fear or anxiety in colleagues was frowned upon and may result in one being told to keep one's B mouth shut.'

Too much chat about fatalities or operational losses and one might be looked upon as lacking moral fibre.

Sam continues,

> 'I found that the longer one was on the Instructional or Operational scene then the more fatalistic one became. Attitude towards pupils was purely factual and fatherly if they wanted to know about an incident. Overall I found that people tended to keep their mouths shut and kept their thoughts to themselves. I never knew of any set policy on such matters.'

Eric Taylor, Corporal in charge of stores at Wing, recalls having the sombre task of clearing out all the belongings from the billetts of those lost in accidents, whilst Fred Capron is only too aware of how the groundcrews on Crash Duty or at the scene of an accident were themselves deeply affected,

> 'My experience of seeing a flying boot with a snapped off leg sticking out of the top was not pleasant and one I shall never forget.'

George Bignell relates a similar tale, relating to a tragic crash which occurred in July 1944, involving Wellington LP314.

> 'About 2a.m the police came banging on my door to say an aircraft had crashed in the cornfield close to 12 Site following Circuits and Bumps Training. We jumped on our bikes and when we arrived we could see the Wellington nose first in the cornfield. The Fire Brigade were already on the scene spraying foam as the aircraft had burst into

flames. Five crewmen died, one still holding the axe with which he tried to break out. I found one airman horribly burnt still strapped into his seat. One crewman survived, he was the tail gunner and was brought out of the rear turret.'

One particular accident that sits firmly in the memory of George Bignell, who witnessed it, occurred on 9th June 1944. George takes up the story,

'The Flight Sergeant instructed me to a hangar to fit a flap relief valve to the Wellington there, (HE 786). This was to prevent new pilots from raising or lowering the flaps too quickly. Whilst I was doing this there was a 'Queen Mary' nearby with a dismantled Tomahawk (AK116)that had been used for practice firing for the gunners. The driver was sitting in the cab reading whilst two WAAF's were tying down the ropes. I had just finished fitting the valve and checked with a LAC who was testing these, when I thought I would have a chat with the driver as I had previously been with a Salvage Unit myself. At that moment, however, someone called out NAAFI so I jumped on my bike and rode off to get my mug of tea.

Before I arrived, there was a loud explosion as a Wellington (HE 854) coming in to land flew off the runway, across the grass just missing a parked Lancaster, and smashed into the Queen Mary. It then carried this into the hangar doors and the whole lot went up in flames. One of the doors fell off, trapping part of the wreck. I tore back to help. The firecrew were pumping in foam, ammunition was flying everywhere and we had to drop down quickly, but we managed to get in close to the wreck. Wing Commander Gardener was also there and he called for the Blood Wagon and we found one of the girls and loaded her on board, but sadly she died before arrival at hospital. As the fuel was flowing so the flames started to spread into the hangar and the wing tip of the aircraft I had been working on caught fire and spread so fast that it too was destroyed. The accident took the lives of two WAAFs, the driver of the Queen Mary and two of the Wellington crew. All that spared me was going for the mug of tea! When I returned to my section they all thought that I had been killed.'

Ken Annable adds that the pilot, fellow Qualified Flight Instructor by the name of Dickie Hubbard, held the aircraft down too long and too low and possibly touched the ground with the retracting undercarriage or propellor tip and swung out of control.

Those killed in this tragic accident were Flying Officer Hubbard and his co-pilot F/O H.Wilkes and three personnel from No.71 Maintenance Unit, namely, Corporal H.Hoare, ACW 1 E.Dickens and LACW A.Reeves.

Unfortunately RAF Wing is noted for another accident of some significance relating to the Martin Baker MB3 aircraft, listed then as 'Experimental Aeroplane No.120' with the Serial Number R2492 and rumoured to be called the 'Whippet'. This aircraft was sent to Wing for trials and first flew on August 31st 1942 with its pilot Captain V.H.Baker,MC,AFC a well known and highly respected test pilot. The tests were supervised by Group Captain Snaith, the Air Ministry Supervisor for Martin Baker and observed by amongst others Air Vice Marshal Linnell and Air Vice Marshal Burton.Tragically, during trials on 12th September, the aircraft crashed killing

The Martin Baker MB3 photographed at Wing shortly before the accident of 12th September 1942 which killed the respected test pilot Captain V.H. Baker MC.AFC. Note the Watch Office in the background (RAF Museum Ref P5751).

Captain Baker.

The Unit Report states,

> 'Capt.Baker had just got airborne, when he had immediate loss of power. In trying to save the aircraft he made a forced landing in a field but hit a tree stump and was killed.'

The subsequent Court Of Inquiry found that,

> 'engine failure (was) due to a broken sleeve drive crank in the engine.'

George Bignell remembers that,

> 'Although nobody was allowed into the aircraft hangar, we were able to see it during its testing time. It was very fast with Captain Baker flying very close at times, shooting up the runway very low.'

On the day of the accident George recalls,

> 'I was doing a modification on dispersals when Captain Baker took off towards Stewkley. I watched him climb then suddenly the engine cut out and he crashed, trying to land.'

John Thornton also remembers the incident,

> 'Two fields from where Morris and I were harvesting, there was a stack of newly threshed straw. The MB3 hit this and burst into flame. 'Bunny' Winter, the bailiff of Cold Harbour Farm, beat us to the crash, but we were too late to rescue Captain Baker in the fierce fire.'

The Unit report actually states that Mr Winter removed the body from the aircraft.

A further accident of tragic consequence involving an aircraft from 26 OTU occurred in the early hours of the 7th August 1943, when a Wellington III, Serial No. X3790 crashed at Winslow as it was returning from a night cross-country exercise. The Unit Report states the following,

> 'The aircraft hit a tree and crashed onto the roof of a house in the High Street(75-77), carried on across the road and after striking the roof of The Chandos Arms, plunged into and demolished a row of four cottages. Fire broke out but was brought under control by the local NFS. Four of the crew were killed and thirteen civilians.'

It appears that the pilot, 22 year old Sergeant Wilfred Davies, decided to return to base because of a malfunction with the bomb sight, but when he made his approach, he found his landing blocked by another aircraft which had 'belly flopped' on the runway. Sgt.Davies tried to complete another circuit of the airfield but failed to gain enough height. The aircraft then hit the tree, lost control and crashed through the series of buildings, ending up in Rose Cottages.

A survivor of the incident, Sheila Barnes, nee Mullis, who lost both her parents, brother and baby sister spoke of the incident at the time of its 50th memorial,

> 'When I came to I managed to crawl out towards a red glow. There was nothing whatsoever left of the house. It was just rubble. It was a traumatic experience. Only in the last five years have we been able to talk about it.'

Jeffrey Harrington was the only member of the crew to survive this tragic accident and his account of events is both fascinating and moving.

> 'We had a practice bombing exercise to complete and it was our joint determination to better our previous record. Everything was to be calculated to the last degree. Obviously knowledge of the winds in the upper air is vital to bombing accuracy and I consulted with the Met man to get the best possible forecast for my flight plan. By the time we had got airborne it was two thirty in the morning of August 7th and our flight progressed normally despite the ungodly hour. John, the Bomb Aimer, asked for the loan of my Navigator's watch to time his bomb strikes better, and I passed it to him. He went down to his position and began his checks on the equipment only to report that the bomb sight had become defective and unusable. We were obliged to abort the run up to the range and altered course to return to base. I was pleased shortly thereafter that we were in the circuit, preparing to land. Everything seemed normal, the approach, the glide path, the conversation and then Taffy said, 'I've got a Red!', which I assumed was a red light or Verey cartridge from Flying Control, as we were just about over the perimeter track and very low, which meant we had to overshoot. I assumed the aircraft in front of us had crashed on the runway and the only place for us was up! I was monitoring my instruments and the altimeter indicated that we were only just clear of the ground and still sinking with a very low airspeed. Taffy called for John to help him 'pull the beggar up' and I noted a painfully slow increase in altitude and airspeed. We clawed at the air and mushed and wallowed our way from the runway and then that was IT! We had been airborne for only twenty minutes and were fully laden.'

The aircraft had overturned during impact and then blown up. As Jeffrey Harrington comments,

> 'Thirteen civilians were killed together with Taffy, Johnny, Jock, Bluey and Wimpy, the crew's cat. How or why I survived I shall never know. I was not strapped in my seat and I can only conclude that as the aircraft blew up I was blown clear to drop in the small gap between spiked iron railings and a corrugated iron hut.'

Jeffrey recalls the moment he came to and the events that followed:

> 'I was lying on what seemed to be either a compost or rubbish heap on an allotment or in someone's back garden. I managed to raise myself up a bit to see over the top of the hut only to be greeted by a great blast of heat and flame as some tank or bomb erupted in the remains of my Wellington bomber. I was totally disorientated; having no idea as to time or place. It was apparent that if I continued to lay where I was I would shortly be engulfed by the conflagration and as I was incapable of scaling the railing, and the iron hut was very hot with a blazing bomber on its far side, I put my whistle to my lips and blew and blew for what seemed an eternity. Above the roaring flames and explosions I heard the sounds of running feet and people shouting. The shouting got closer and then careful hands eased me over the railings. Anxious, cautious people supported me up the path of a little cottage and into the parlour. In

common with most aircrew of my acquaintance, I had a dread, almost a phobia I suppose, of being brought down over Germany. We had been bombarded with stories of downed airmen being manhandled and even lynched in these circumstances, and this fear must have been in the forefront of my thoughts when I asked,

'Where am I?'

'Look,' I managed to say, though I've no idea what my voice sounded like as I had lost part of my lips to the hot metal of my whistle that was attached to my battledress collar, 'Just tell me which country I am in. Is this England?" I ought to have known, for I was the navigator but honestly, I didn't have a clue!'

Jeffrey was soon taken in an ambulance by an RAF medical team to the burns ward of Princess Mary's Hospital at Halton. He ended up with a face mask dressing with three slits and a tube in one to syphon fluids and both hands and lower arms were in splints to stop his fingers from contracting. His right leg was bandaged and there were numerous bandages over his head and neck.

The accident was commemorated with with a 50th anniversary memorial service at St Laurence's Church, Winslow in 1993 and a plaque in memory of those who died was unveiled.

It reads,

'To the memory of those Winslow residents, evacuees, and air crew who lost their lives when a Wellington bomber returning to Horwood Airfield crashed on this site on 7th August 1943."

The Court Of Inquiry set up under Air Vice Marshall H.K.Thorold the Commanding Officer of 92 Group bluntly declared,

'The accident was due to the pilot not concentrating on his instruments, and therefore allowing the aircraft to lose height.'

Those who perished were:

Thomas Cox, publican.

Israel and Annie Goldberg, their daughter Lottie Hoberman and grandson Victor Hoberman, ironically all evacuees from London.

William Hawkins and wife Nora.

Stephen Mullis, wife Doris, son Terence aged ten and daughter Kathleen aged just five months.

Tom Paintin and son Donald.

Sgt. Wilfred Davies, Pilot.

Sgt. Clive Feitz, front Air Gunner. (Royal Australian Air Force).

Sgt. John McKeon, Wireless Operator.

Sgt. John Sowter, rear Air Gunner.

In Appendix 1, I have compiled details of the many accidents involving aircraft from 26 OTU which resulted in fatalities and/or loss of aircraft. The latter could be replaced, of course, but the loss of so many young men before they even experienced actual operational flying was undoubtedly a disaster in itself and commonplace in virtually all OTUs.

As well as the more serious accidents, many minor incidents also occurred where injuries were slight or not suffered at all and aircraft received a lesser amount of damage. I have not compiled an exhaustive list of these, although I am sure they evoke vivid memories for those involved, as indeed the following examples show.

Edward Eyres flew as Navigator at Wing from December 1943 to April 1944 and recalls an accident which, thankfully, did not result in any fatalities nor indeed serious injury. He recalls,

> 'I'm afraid we wrote off (HE) 479 on 20th February '44. The Starboard engine cut out on take off and we landed on the tarmac in front of Flying Control. They said we got out of that aircraft in 4 seconds flat! As we came in after going round the circuit at 0ft on one engine they tried to tell us to land on the grass (mud!) but as we touched the tarmac she caught fire at the tail and fire came sweeping up the aircraft! Fortunately, I had managed to ditch the astro-dome and we shot out like corks out of a bottle! The only injury was self inflicted when Wattie Swan the Rear Gunner went back for his helmet and got his eyebrows singed for his pains.
>
> The C.O. asked why we didn't use the fire extinguisher – if we had I shouldn't be writing this! – but he gave us a week's leave.'

The official report relating to this incident names the pilot as F/Sgt J.S.Wood. As with the majority of accidents the pilot's inexperience was stated to be the cause. John Streeter witnessed another accident at Wing airfield that did not end in tragedy,

> 'I had a good view of one Wimpey coming in to land with 'cart' trouble. The port leg collapsed on touch down and it was running on starboard for a while. It then swung round heading for a hangar but as it hit the perimeter track the starboard leg broke and it finished up just outside the hangar ready to be jacked up and wheeled in. I remember all the 'bods' running out of the opposite end of the hangar!'

CHAPTER 6
On the Ground

As already stated the role of the ground crews and specialist tradesmen was vital in ensuring aircraft were in a fit state to take to the air. Hours were long, as Flight Mechanic Rex Austen states,

> 'Normally we worked 0730 – 1930 hours'.

The duties for a Flight Mechanic took place on 'the Flights' at the dispersal pans making daily inspections and assisting in engine starting and they were accompanied by Riggers, ie airframe mechanics or fitters. Engine Fitters were employed on major inspections which mainly involved engine changes. The team would have included a Corporal plus two or three others. Fred Capron recalls his team working 0800 to 1800 hours although there were occasions when maximising the number of serviceable aircraft was necessary, for example, at the time of the 1000 bomber raids, requiring extended shifts 0730 to 2200 hours for six days and 0730 until 1300 on the seventh. The half day was staggered so that maintenance was carried out over the seven days.

Fred remembers that,

> 'Even on the half day off many went home (mainly to London) and back in the 11 hours free time.'

After major servicing like an engine change the tradesmen, usually an Engine Fitter, accompanied the pilot carrying out flight check.

Fred recalls,

> 'We had to take parachutes because of regulations but they were useless at the low heights that we flew. Because of this and the number of accidents that occurred during training the tradesmen, despite their admiration of the aircrews, had a saying, 'only fools and pigeons fly'.'

Rex Austen remembers his duties beginning with,

> 'sweeping and cleaning out drip trays in Hangar 1. Later I was allowed to help with plug changes on the Wimpeys.'

Rex also took part in air tests and vividly recalls the first,

> 'I had my first flight in a Wimpey from Wing, just the pilot and myself, I believe it was the Wing Commander. I remember sitting on the main spar prior to take off- I was a bit wary, being a 'sprog', of these officers with multiple rings on their sleeve. However he beckoned me up into the cockpit where I stood as we raced down the runway. We were up about 20 minutes over the lovely countryside. He once pointed at the instruments, I just nodded, I hadn't a clue at that time as to whether everything was

Ground Crew standing beside a visiting Stirling LJ 635. LAC Fred Capron can be seen far left. Third from the left is Corporal Saxby. (F.C.)

normal or not, but it was a great experience.'

Armourer John Streeter also remembers his first Air Test,

'I worked with another armourer named 'Tich' Armstrong and we used to service front and rear turrets and the guns. On several occasions we went up on Air Tests with parachute and harness and I always remember my first one. I was in the rear turret when the pilot did a bit of 'corkscrewing' and my mate was laughing his head off. He didn't tell me what would be going on during these short test flights but I did enjoy them when the weather was good.'

Those involved in these Air Tests seem to have extraordinary clear memories of them. Here Corporal George Bignell recounts one particular test flight,

'I was in the front gun turret, the only seat left. After take off, which I thought was very short, the pilot started to bank very quickly, then he did the usual tests with all the controls. Then we came in very smoothly, hardly feeling the wheels touch, on to the dispersal to check over the parts. Going round the starboard side there was a whole length of fabric hanging down the side from the cockpit to part way down the fuselage. When I showed the pilot he said, 'The bloody thing must be rotten. I only put it in a dive at about 140mph!' It was a good job we landed OK – we didn't have one parachute between us.'

Rex Austen mentioned that he was wary of mixing with the aircrews. The main contact between the tradesmen and the aircrew would have been at dispersals with the latter being transported out to the aircraft parked on the perimeter of the airfield. The relationship would be best described as a quiet admiration for each other, Fred Capron suggests,

'The Aircrew recognised the conditions in which Mechanics worked including night work. The tradesmen recognised the difficulties of the training programme for Aircrews.'

The fact that on the Air Tests both flew together no doubt cemented the relationship between the two groups, as each relied on the other.

There was a greater distance between the tradesmen and the General Duties Airmen, almost one of disdain. The latter would carry out mundane tasks like toilet and waste disposal with a substantial difference in pay. Fred Capron recalls how this relationship changed,

'Originally we were placed on domestic sites in trades or like trades. The threat of enemy paratroopers wiping out one site of say Fitters would result in the Station becoming almost non-operational. This was all changed so that huts on the sites contained a multiplicity of trades and job holders. Consequently relationships improved greatly.'

Groundcrew were often required to attend training courses in other parts of the country, thus George Bignell recalls a week's course with a Corporal Bird near Brooklands racetrack where Wellingtons were being built at four a day.

'We had to work with the staff all day, first on the fuselage, then the undercarriage before installing petrol tanks etc.'

George then returned to Wing and joined a newly set up Modifications Unit under Wing

Commander Gardner, along with a Flight Sergeant Steele, Corporals Holmes and Viddes and LACs Wordman, Humphrey, Wicks and Cresswell. Amongst the WAAFs on this Unit was ACW Burton.

'We had to work hard because there were so many modifications to do, such as the installation of Second pilot controls, chutes for each aircraft to drop leaflets from , flap relief valves etc. One tricky job we had was to remove the levers which operated the small petrol tanks used when the fuel was low and reposition these controls to the side of the second pilot's seat so he could operate them in an emergency without needing to leave his seat.'

One memorable job involved modifications to a Dakota used by Field Marshall Montgomery.

'This was to fit a special aerial for communication. The aircraft was fitted out with a bedroom, desk, phones, radio and big easy chairs. No-one was allowed in the aircraft or even the hangar other than its own particular crew and Corporals Bignell and Ashby.'

Fred Capron was also involved in modifications and certain aspects of this work are recalled.

'To provide more power for the Wellington, the Pegasus single bank nine cylinder engine was replaced by the double bank fourteen cylinder Hercules engine. This caused problems when the engine mounting rings started to develop cracks. The new engine was heavier and protruded further forward so all the Wellingtons were grounded until new thicker mounting rings arrived and were fitted. Another modification was needed to prevent enemy aircraft spotting radial engined aircraft by the exhaust ring heat glow. A special paint was developed to reduce the glow and we had to paint this on.'

The difficulty of some of the jobs required the fitters to use their skills to make their own tools in the workshops to cope with the task in hand.

Fred recalls that nothing was wasted when servicing an aircraft,

'During major servicing the aircraft had to be emptied of fuel. However, the Bowser could not completely empty the tanks so the last 40 gallons or so were emptied into small open wheelbarrow-like trolleys and was then used to clean the engine and bulkheads.'

Specialists in certain fields were also found on the airfield and Fred remembers one in particular.

'In the propeller bay was a Corporal running his own one-man department carrying out any

Fred Capron again, working on the engine of a Wellington. (F.C.)

work necessary on that part of the aircraft. Being a Corporal he was able to get airmen to lift the 'props on to jigs for him to carry out his work. He was an expert, and working alone he was able to develop a sideline – making wooden toys. He had a spray gun and unlimited supplies of various colours of cellulose paint. Toys were not easy to come by in the shops so he was particularly busy at Christmas.'

With aircraft arriving regularly from squadrons, Maintenance Units and other OTUs, ensuring they were in good condition put pressure upon the groundcrews to the extent that in October 1942 a Special Servicing Flight was set up. Their function was to bring the serviceability of aircraft up to a higher percentage and according to the ORB this proved successful. Not only did aircraft arrive at 26 OTU on a regular basis, but they also moved on as the following example shows. It would be interesting to consider the number of groundcrew who were involved with maintaining the condition of this aircraft during its lifetime.

WELLINGTON MARK 1C R1224

Taken On Charge	5.11.40	22 MU
	28.11.40	12 OTU
	29.11.40	15 OTU
	8. 7.41	Vickers
	20.10.41	12 MU
	22.10.41	23 MU

– where it was involved in bombing operations over Germany, as well as training. This aircraft, whilst at Wing was also involved in an accident in early February 1943 when during taxying its tail struck an oil bearer, despite the pilot having guidance via signals from the groundcrew. According to the Unit Report, the groundcrew failed to check for obstacles whilst the pilot was considered partially to blame for turning the aircraft carelessly and quickly. The result of this was that the aircraft was sent for repairs, returning to Wing on 27th February.

	16.3.43	14 OTU
	8.9.43	28 OTU
Struck Off Charge	31.3.44	

That the aircraft survived for nearly four years is surprising considering the number of accidents at OTUS and the fact that it took part in the raids in September 1942, details of which can be found in a later chapter. Perhaps in part this is testament to the sterling work of the crews on the ground.

CHAPTER 7
On yer Bike

Of all the vital pieces of equipment required by personnel at Wing, the bicycle came high on the list. It seems everyone had a bike, which enabled them to travel from the domestic sites to their place of work and other areas of the airfield, and which also shortened the journey to the local hostelries during an evening out. Fred Capron tells of the importance of the bike in relation to periods of leave,

Modelling the typical station cycle is Canadian Pilot 'Chick' Chigwidden snapped outside one of the Domestic Sites on the Cublington Road. (J.Bo.)

'The leave some of us enjoyed could be 11 hours, one day, 48 hours or 7 days. Personnel going on leave were likely to cycle to either Leighton Buzzard or Aylesbury railway station. The side of the former was a mass of bicycles. Your bicycle was identified by a number in white paint daubed on the frame. After leave, retrieving your bike was a nightmare as they were entangled like barbed wire, so many of us got friendly with a number of Leighton Buzzard residents, who did not live too far from the station. They allowed us to leave our bikes in their gardens or passages etc. On return from leave on a cold night many would provide us with a hot drink and with this inside us and the ride up the hill to Wing village we were soon warm. Often, because of a shortage of money or a lack of supply of batteries some of us did not have lights so those who did convoyed the others back to camp. I don't recall any convictions or airmen placed on charge'.

Jack Robinson, a trainee signaller at the Unit from February to November 1945, was grateful for his bicycle when it came to leave time.

'As my home at that time was in Heston, Middlesex I was able to make weekly visits, cycling down to Leighton Buzzard station and putting my bike with, it seemed, hundreds of others, in the Left Luggage Office, for 6d. The difficulty was trying to identify it on the Sunday night at 11pm.'

Fred Capron remembers that the bikes were mainly Raleigh ladies' cycles, and they were undoubtedly treasured, especially when used to speed up the journey to the local pubs. Sam Lawton recalls that a visit to The Sportsman in Wing, where 'mine host' was one Pat Pattendon, needed,

'a swing to port when cycling from the airfield'.

Not everyone at the Camp was familiar with riding a bike, as Eric Taylor remembers,

'One Aircraftman 2nd Class was unable to master riding a bike so I taught him, but not without some difficulty. On one occasion I set him off riding to Cublington church only to see him fall off into the ditch.'

The personnel obviously enjoyed the hospitality offered at the local pubs and many had their favourites amongst those in Wing, Stewkley and Cublington, whilst some ventured slightly further afield. Cliff Stewart considers that,

'One reason for going to so many different pubs was that it was not unusual for them to run out of beer.'

Like many, Cliff has pleasant memories of the pubs.

'In those days, village pubs in particular were very friendly places. Everyone talked to everybody else and you could always join in a game of darts or skittles and the beer was so weak you could drink all night. I recall winning a live duck in a raffle at the pub on the Stewkley Road, just before Christmas 1944. We took it back to the camp and kept it in a pen made up of wire bedsteads, feeding it up at night, or so we thought, on scraps of bread. The diet didn't seem to suit since it started to look thinner every day. Finally we gave it the chop, literally, with a large knife and had it for supper one night!'

Sam Lawton fondly remembers,

'Alma the assistant Black & Tan server at The Bell in Leighton Buzzard and Mrs Keppy that lovely lady 'Landlord' of the pub alongside the canal at Cheddington, (possibly The Duke Of Wellington), who used to provide us with the odd meal, sheer luxury for five bob a time.'

No doubt he speaks for all when he states,

'These lovely people helped to make war-time life 'liveable' for many hundreds of aircrew lads who didn't know whether they would still be extant next week or even the next morning.'

The Camp dances were also very popular with the Camp having it's own band, whilst the WAAFs organised dances in their own Mess, (the first of these on the 25th January 1943, in Fancy Dress!) to add to the entertainments on offer. Ken Annable remembers there being a weekly dance in the village hall in Wing, as does Australian Allan Hardwicke, who has an abiding memory of the 'Cabbage Dance', whatever that was. He also took great delight in,

'teaching Air Traffic WAAFs Aussie slang.'

Leighton Buzzard was something of a hot spot, it seems, with Keith McClean recalling regular dances at The Old Vic and The Corn Exchange and Ken Annable considering it commonplace to,

'walk a girl to Leighton Buzzard and then back to the airfield.'

Another favourite venue was the ballroom above the Co-op which Ron Stotter certainly frequented, remembering that the return to Camp led to a scramble for Station bicycles which were left in a pile outside.

'Often the bike we took was not our own, but it was a Station bike and the true ownership would be sorted out the next day.'

Another of Ron's memories concerns the return of the WAAF's to their site after an evening out.

'The forbidding appearance of the WAAF Sergeant would be noticeable standing outside the WAAF quarters waiting for her charges to return. She was making sure that no harm would befall her girls and we were lucky indeed to get a goodnight kiss!'

George Bignell sallied forth in the opposite direction to Leighton Buzzard and recalls,

'working passes to attend dances at Whitchurch and Oving.'

It was following one of these that he remembers,

'returning one evening to find my Unit repairing a puncture on a Wellington.'

The periods of leave were of great importance enabling personnel to visit families and sweethearts. Many of those stationed at Wing came from the London area so the railway network was a vital link.

'Many would have found it difficult to afford the travel costs but for the laxity and goodwill shown to servicemen by the railway staff,'

states Fred Capron who was grateful for the assistance given on his journey to Edgware.

'I usually caught the 1703 or 1724 from Leighton Buzzard to Watford Junction, then a 142 bus to home. Returning, however, to ensure getting a seat, it was Northern Line to Euston to get a train back – all on a Leighton Buzzard to Watford return ticket. Servicemen enjoyed a special status and ticket collectors were happy to be given any ticket.'

Ken Meen, trainee Navigator, would certainly agree with Fred's sentiments.

'One night I arrived at Euston late to find that my normal train had gone and none were running until the next morning. Panic set in, as I was down to fly next morning early. The station staff at Euston were most helpful and told me a troop train left at 8pm to Oxford and always stopped at Winslow for water, within walking distance to Wing! I checked with the driver of the train who said that he would be stopping for water as usual. A few shillings made doubly certain he would! I mentioned this to a few people and the next week about ten got off at Winslow. This went on for a few weeks with the numbers rising each time. Then came the crunch. One week when I checked with the driver he told me he had a large engine on and would not be stopping. A hurried conference and a collection which amounted to about a fortnight's pay made the driver reconsider. He soon felt that he ought to stop for water after all!'

Donald Sykes, at the Unit for Pilot training from October 1942 February 1943, remembers an even more unusual incident relating to transport matters.

'At Christmas 1942 we were informed that we should stay in camp and not use public transport. However the temptation was too great and with home only in Watford, three of us set off to hitch-hike. After an hour or more without luck we were on the point of giving up, when a hearse, complete with coffin, stopped and took us as far as Berkhamsted!'

On returning late from leave Fred Capron recalls a little ruse which ensured a bite to eat before returning to billets.

'We would illegally join the queue of those on night flying duty for their late supper. The cookhouse staff turned a blind eye because they would see by our clean uniforms that we were not on night flying.'

The food, however, was not highly recommended.

'In common with those in civvy street we always felt hungry. The food was generally poor although this was not the fault of the cookhouse staff who like the rest of the country 'had to make do'. The most deplorable meal was once a week for breakfast. It was fish paste mixed with mashed potato and then baked or grilled. It tasted horrible. The tea was also dreadful, being laced with bromide! The NAAFI tea was slightly better.'

As time progressed the food did improve, with bacon and eggs for Sunday breakfast and the introduction of salad, as fresh produce became more plentiful. Much of the fruit and vegetables was grown on the Ascott Estate gardens, with one particular field east of and adjacent to the kennels, being ploughed up for the purpose of producing cabbages. Wally Willis, one of six gardeners working on the estate at the time, called this plot 'Hitler's Patch', a name still used today.

One occasion when the food was considerably better was the Annual Christmas Dinner – a real treat and an occasion to bring the Unit together. As can be seen from the Menu for the

1942 Dinner, a real effort was made to provide the best possible meal that circumstances allowed. It was even served in customary fashion by the Officers just to add that little bit extra!

Christmas, 1942.

AIRMEN AND W.A.A.F. MESS

ROYAL AIR FORCE ... ... 26 O.T.U., WING

MENU

Kidney Soup.

Roast Norfolk Turkey.

Ham. Stuffing.

Roast Potatoes. Brussels Sprouts.

Sauce.

Xmas Pudding.

Brandy Sauce.

Mince Pies.

Apples.

Beer. Minerals. Cigarettes.

Merry Christmas

The menu from the 1942 Christmas Dinner served in the Airmen's and WAAF Mess on the Communal Site.

As the map of the airfield clearly shows, there were 13 domestic sites spread along the Wing to Cublington road and in the fields adjacent. Within each site there were up to 20 huts along with latrines and ablutions, a picket post and one or two air raid shelters. The huts were divided into officers', sergeants' and airmen's quarters. Jeffrey Harrington remembers,

> 'The living quarters were dispersed in a seemingly haphazard manner, with only spartan sanitary facilities nearby. We had to traipse to the Mess for hot water which was a not inconsiderable distance.'

It certainly wasn't especially for those stuck out in the fields in Sites 6,7 or 12!

The WAAFs had a similar site of their own nearer to Wing village on the same road, with the same facilities, much of which is still standing today.

When asked what he remembers about Wing, Rex Austen has a lasting impression of,

> 'the lovely countryside, hot summer days, Bomber Command filling the skies with sound,' and, less romantically, 'the smell of the Elsans in the latrines!'

He also recalls the considerable distance from the Nissen Huts to the hangars, again underlining the value of the good old bike. The huts themselves were typical of the period with hollow clad, asbestos type walls and metal window frames, officially referred to as 16017/40, the latter reference being the date of the design. They were heated by a slow combustion stove situated in the centre. Fred Capron remembers,

> 'Those nearest the stove roasted whilst in winter those nearest the doors froze. When the fire needed lighting the first arrival back in the evening had the responsibility.'

Eric Taylor remembers one Sergeant on Number 4 Site who kept the stove alight constantly. Coke was rationed to a degree so it might have been useful to have become familiar with those in charge of it.

John Boxall has clear memories of the cold winter of 1945/46 and how he and his colleagues ensured they kept warm.

> 'We had the single iron heating stove in the middle of the hut and a limited supply of coke, which with a bit of luck could be supplemented with a little extra from the coke store, (which happened to be adjacent to our site), if you could make or find a hole under the wire surround. Tuesday was the day the weekly ration was issued and if possible, one person was left in the hut on that day to prevent raiding parties from other huts stealing your ration. Most nights one's overcoat was used as a top blanket. As personnel were posted, one moved one's bed space nearer to the stove before the new inmates arrived.'

Eric Taylor recalls a Corporal Tinker, an ex-mining Geordie, who looked after the coke and coal in the fuel compounds.

> 'He was able to look at a pile of coal and say exactly how much was there.'

He also recalls how men, including airmen, would be grabbed for coal fatigues. They would shovel the coal or coke onto a lorry which the Corporal and a WAAF driver would distribute around the Camp. When Eric was asked to cover for the Corporal he soon worked out that,

> 'coke was easier to carry than coal.'

Hugh Richards, a commissioned Wireless Operator/Air Gunner who was with the Unit from February 1944 adds another tale relating to that important commodity – coal!!

> 'On a very cold day in early February, a number of Officers were issued with overalls and ordered to go by truck to a coal dump and bag up fuel for the Officers' Quarters. You can imagine whose Hut ended up with the biggest stock!'

Ken Meen was posted to Wing as a Sergeant Navigator on Christmas Eve 1944 and has vivid memories of a desperately cold winter.

> 'I was in hut 283 on No.9 Site and it was bitterly cold with no heating or hot water on the Site. It was nearly a mile's walk to the Mess to get washed and shaved. We drew extra clothing – three sets of vests, long pants, jersey and gloves. There was also no heating in the classrooms so we often wore flying kit in these.'

One memory of the Domestic Sites Fred Capron has is the supply of mushrooms in the fields which were collected and taken home when on leave. Apparently the huts were inspected once a week but Fred cannot remember any criticism of his particular billet. John Boxall recalls,

> 'Being a training establishment we had to fold and form the blankets to the standard layout each morning and occasionally had to lay out kit for kit inspections. Similarly we had a 'bull' night cleaning the hut which was checked and inspected by a senior officer before we could stand down. A small square of blanket under each foot produced highly polished lino and reduced the effort needed on these nights.'

Everyday cleanliness and hygiene was essential, especially when living in a hut with a number of others. Washing occurred in the communal wash-house and Fred Capron remarks,

> 'Once you were in, you could not see others for steam.'

John Boxall comments,

> 'The ablution standards were pretty poor, but fortunately I was an early riser so my ablutions were completed before the hot water ran out.'

In order for clothes to be cleaned all laundry was tied up in a towel, labelled with a list of items, name, rank, number and location and that is how it was returned. Most personnel took much of their washing home when on leave, however.

On the Communal Site, opposite the main entrance to the airfield, which included the Dining Rooms, Cinema, Gymnasium, Church, NAAFI and various stores, personnel could make use of a barber, tailor and shoemaker as well as a Post Office.

The Station also had medical facilities, with a hospital site situated close to the village of Cublington, some distance from the airfield proper. Here worked the medical team including at least one doctor and a dental surgeon.

Fred Capron again,

> 'The dentist had a sadistic sense of humour. On the door of his surgery was a large hand-drawn cartoon depicting a huge pneumatic drill being used on a small tooth. Alongside was a beckoning finger under which were the words 'COME IN' boldly displayed.'

Crew 'team' photo including John Boxall (extreme left) beside Wellington ??965. (J.Bo.)

Dental Surgery (right) at the Hospital Site photographed in 1997. Note the original décor. (author)

Rex Austen recalls that one M.O. was rather unsympathetic on an occasion when he burnt his hand,

> 'Next morning I had an enormous blister on the back of my hand so naturally I 'went sick'. The M.O. tore me off a right strip, and threatened that I ought to be 'on charge for not reporting sick earlier."

The buildings of the 'Sick Quarters' are still standing today, just – as can be seen in the photographs. The internal walls of the main ward and offices still display the cream paintwork with a green band and Arthur Read pointed out to me the dental surgery, where he recalls having a tooth extracted when a boy. He also remembers how, 'many of those who lived too far away to travel home on 48 hour leave, especially those from Scotland, enjoyed having the time to spend on the gardens in the hospital site grounds.'

Behind the main ward and beyond the car park is a grassy bank on which Arthur recalls a copy of the Unit badge being cut into the turf.

As well as the chance to enjoy time off-camp, there were also plenty of opportunities for the sport-minded at the Unit itself. On the communal site was the gymnasium and squash courts whilst rugby, football and cricket were all keenly played against teams from around the locality. Sam Lawton, being an enthusiastic cricketer was more than happy to organise a team. This proved to be fruitful for Sam both at work and play.

Inside the main ward of the Hospital Site in 1997. (author)

The only brick built building on the Hospital Site 1997. (author)

'I was put in unofficial control of an Australian group of about sixteen Trainee Wireless Operator/Air Gunners who had not yet been crewed-up.They were reported to have been almost out of control due to having been mucked about whilst being transported to Wing via the USA from their homeland.

After having an hour or two speaking to the lads mainly on cricketing matters and dropping a few names – Don Bradman, Stan McCabe, Bill Woodfull plus Harold Larwood, Wally Hammond, Maurice Leyland (from the England side), I began to realise they were just about as frustrated as I was at that time. So I obtained permission to approach Wing Cricket Club and arranged a bit of practice for them. From that day on no-one had an ounce of trouble from the very many Australian Aircrew trainees who passed through Wing. The names of the instructors were known to the Aussie trainees before they arrived. The Aussie's grapevine was very efficient.'

One name remembered with fondness by Sam and no doubt other 26 OTU cricketers, is that of Harry Pitchford, the groundsman at the cricket club, who can be seen in the

The dilapidated remains of a domestic building on the Hospital Site. (author)

Cricketers from staff member of C and D Flights 26 OTU.
Back left to right: F/Sgt Renshaw, F/Lt Gorrie, F/O Sam Lawton, ? Ken Annable, F/Lt Chaldecott, unknown.
Front left to right: W/O Ron Soutar, F/Sgt Stan (Gabbie) Garbutt, unknown, Cpl Franky Bell, Harry Pitchford, Cpl Jack Roberts. Note the last two characters listed appear in both cricket line-ups. (F.C.)

RAF Wing Cricket Club – July 1944 probably taken at Ascott.
Back left to right: Cpl Barry Dewhurst, unknown, unknown, unknown, Sgt Vivienne Russell, unknown, unknown, F/Lt Freddie Cramp.
Front left to right: LAC Percy Savage, F/Lt Greenwood, Sgt Jack Roberts, P/O/ Jack Bates, Harry Pitchford – groundsman. (J.Ba.)

photograph, along with Sam taken sometime in 1943/44.

Jack Bates was posted to 26 OTU in March 1944 as Acting Pilot Officer assigned to the Engineering Section. He too has found memories of the cricket played at Ascott.

> 'The Station cricket team had full use of the beautiful Ascott House ground. I played there at every opportunity and even met my wife there in her capacity as scorer. She was a WAAF Sergeant in Accounts – Vivienne Russell. The PT Instructor F/O Greenwood (Yorkshireman – slow left arm bowler) and his Sergeant, Jack Roberts, had assembled a very good side. Included in this were F/L Fred Cramp and LAC Percy Savage amongst others.'

Jack also remembers Harry Pitchford, who was renowned for his superb pitches and outfield, whilst he also recalls some interesting opposition.

> 'One of our opposing teams was 60 Group (Signals) whose captain was Eddie Hapgood, the Arsenal and England footballer. I asked him how, at left back, he dealt with Stanley Matthews. His answer was, 'not to let him have the ball.' Another team we played was made up of local farmers and included three one-armed players. In spite of their apparent handicap, they were combative and competent performers in both batting and bowling.'

A strong football team also developed at R.A.F. Wing. Fred Capron was a member of the team which enjoyed great success in the 1944/45 season playing against other R.A.F. stations and local sides.

> 'We had a strong team which at one time included Ivor Broadis, the England international who played for Spurs and Manchester City and two Wycombe Wanderers players, George Jackson and Arthur Hallwood. I played at centre-half and in one game, the semi-final of the Beds & Bucks Cup, we beat Luton Town 3-1. Playing for Luton was a Wing lad by the name of Woolhead who later became the landlord at The Cock. After the game the Luton manager George Martin signed me on.'

It is apparent from the match details for that season kindly supplied by Fred, that the team went on to win the Beds & Bucks Cup.

Fred remembers that after matches he would cycle in the team kit to the washhouse on the Communal Site to shower and how large crowds would watch the games, especially those played in the evening or late afternoon. Dick Revill recalls his PT Instructor at the Unit as Sergeant Bill Williams, later to become England goalkeeper.

Eric Taylor assures me that rugby was also particularly popular with the pitches for both football and rugby being situated in the field opposite Number 5 Site.

George Bignell is proud of his contribution to the Station Darts team which was also very successful in local competitions.

The ORB makes reference to an even wider range of sporting activities played at one time or another by personnel in the Unit. Hockey matches were played at Ascott, whilst tennis, boxing, badminton and netball were enjoyed, along with fencing and even fishing competitions.

R.A.F. WING STATION XI

SEASON 1944 - 45

DATE	OPPONENTS	VENUE	FOR	AGAINST	REMARKS
-	R.A.F. Chipping Warden	A	6	0	
-	R.A.F. Silverstone	A	1	0	
-	R.A.F. Chipping Norton	A	3	3	
-	R.A.F. Leighton Buzzard	A	1	0	Eddie Hapgood's XI
-	L.M.S. Bletchley	H	8	4	
-	R.A.F. Upper Heyford	H	6	2	
-	R.A.F. Leighton Buzzard	H	10	1	Eddie Hapgood's XI
-	R.A.F. Husband Bosworth	A	1	5	Bomber Command 92 Group K.O. tournament
-	L.M.S. Bletchley	A	3	1	
-	Wing Village	H	3	0	
Wed. 7.3.45*	Luton Town XI	H	3	1	Beds/Bucks Cup semi-final
-	London Brick Company	H	4	2	
-	Vauxhall Motors	A	2	4	
-	R.A.F. Dunstable	H	5	2	
Good Friday 30.3.45	Luton T. Amateurs	A	1	0	Beds/Bucks Cup Final played on Leighton Buzzard Town F.C.'s ground

*In this game a Wing Villager Woolhead played centre forward for Luton Town.

Played	Won	Drawn	Lost	For	Against
15	12	1	2	57	25

The writer apologies for the missing dates and not being able to identify the Cup round matches prior to the Semi-Final.

The small number of games recorded is due to three main reasons:

1: Pre-occupation of the players during a crucial period of the war.

2: Many of the available dates were taken up by internal (R.A.F. Wing personnel only) competitions. There were at least two knock out competitions staged during this season.

3: If by chance, and it is unlikely, that games were not recorded in the above, it could only be that I was on leave or playing for Luton Town.

Match details for the RAF Wing Football XI during 1944/45 season, compiled by Fred Capron.

Another of the many popular sports enjoyed at RAF Wing was tug o' war, here seen taking place on the Station sports field. (F.C.)

Sports Day 1944 – Jack Bates wins the 440 yards. (J.Ba.)

John Whitworth DFC formed a Station Golf team with F/O Peter Atkins and F/O Greenwood, who was Sports Officer at Wing. Matches were played at Leighton Buzzard Golf Club against their hosts and a team from Dunstable Golf Club, whilst in January 1944 a Sports tournament took place at Wing against teams from RAF Hornchurch. The visitors were made most welcome and enjoyed considerable hospitality. Football, rugby and hockey matches were played on this occasion.

One sport at which the Unit excelled was Canadian Softball, with the 26 OTU team competing in the finals of a national tournament held in Hyde Park in September 1943. No doubt the team was made up from the numerous Royal Canadian Air Force personnel training at 26 OTU.

There is little doubt then, that every effort was made to provide a comfortable and interesting environment for personnel at the Unit especially as none knew exactly what might be awaiting them from day to day. In some ways it is difficult to appreciate that this was war time, with the work in progress an important cog in the wheel of the nation's fighting machine.

Relationships bonded in such an environment and in such extreme circumstances were quite unique and in many cases unforgettable; the comradeship, as George Bignell remarks was simply, 'wonderful'.

John Streeter comments in similar vein,

> 'comradeship will always exist in the Forces but not with quite such a strong bond as then.'

Two views of the gymnasium situated on the Communal site. The original wooden floor including some of the badminton court markings still exists, although at the time the picture was taken the building housed farm machinery. (author)

CHAPTER 8
26 OTU in Action

Perhaps the most important period in the short history of 26 OTU is that in which the Unit saw 'action' during 1942, when it contributed both aircraft and crews to the 1000 Plan Raids.

It was on the 30th May 1942 that Commander In Chief Sir Arthur Harris and his close staff made the decision, in the underground office of Bomber Command Headquarters at High Wycombe, to bomb Cologne with a force of 1000 bomber aircraft.

It was a major decision giving fruition to Harris's idea of massive, rapid assault offensives utilising vast numbers of aircraft to deliver a shattering blow to Germany and it is still considered today as one of the most controversial decisions of the War.

The 1000 Plan, as it was known, required massive organisation. Earlier in May, Air Vice Marshall Saundby had begun to review the number of aircraft and crews available and the first plan of action was considered by Chief Of Air Staff Sir Charles Portal, who in turn approached Prime Minister Winston Churchill. By the 20th of the month official approval was received.

To meet the number of aircraft required, Saundby was to draw from Main Bomber Squadrons and Heavy Conversion Units some 678 aircraft whilst OTUs and sundry training units eventually provided 369. Crews were made up of experienced flyers and advanced trainees, not all of whom were to return.

The make up of the Force was as follows:

1 Group	–	100 aircraft
3 Group	–	160
4 Group	–	130
5 Group	–	95
91 Group	–	200
92 Group	–	120
Coastal Command	–	250
Flying Training Command	–	21

In effect the number of aircraft actually serviceable for the first raid was 1047, with 92 Group for example, only in fact providing 114 aircraft.

Eight crews from 26 OTU were involved whilst a further 12 aircraft from the Unit were crewed by members of 22 and 27 OTUs.

Sadly as far as 26 OTU is concerned three aircraft were reported missing from this first raid, whilst two crashed on return. Full details of the aircraft and their crews are included later in this chapter.

An insight into the preparations for crew members is given by Ralph Edwards, later to become Squadron Leader and receive the Distinguished Service Order. He was a member of a 26 OTU crew and in his book, 'In The Thick Of It' he vividly recalls the time.

> 'Towards the end of May 1942 flying training was suspended suddenly and instructional staff were ordered to form their men – at all stages of training – into complete crews; pilots, navigators, wireless operators and front and rear gunners. Rumours were rife – What was happening? Was an invasion planned? On 27th May aircrews were ordered to fly their aircraft to a newly constructed aerodrome at Graveley, near St Neots. We were to be accommodated in Nissen huts. Crews arriving in the later hours were not so fortunate; they had to sleep on floors and store their clothing and equipment in the chicken huts of a nearby farm. We settled in as best we could under the cramped circumstances still wondering what was in the wind. All we knew was that we were to be under the command of Wing Commander Biggs, the Chief Flying Instructor at Cheddington.'

At 1800 hours on the 30th May the aircrews were called to attend a briefing. They were told,

> 'Gentlemen you are privileged to take part in a special operation tonight, a momentous occasion. One thousand bombers will be attacking a single target. The target is Cologne.'

In fact, the original plan for the first raid targeted Hamburg and was to take place on the 26th May, only for the weather to force a cancellation and a change of date and target.

Squadron Leader Edwards continues,

> 'Briefing continued with details about strategy. The night had been carefully chosen: there was a full moon with good visibility. Time for take-off was 2300 hours and we were due over the target at 0100 hours. The duration of the raid was to be compressed into 90 minutes, with the bomber force sent off in a continuous stream along a common route. We would thus pass through a minimum number of radar-controlled night fighter boxes, which in turn would reduce the number of possible interceptions; the fighter controllers could only direct a maximum of six potential interceptions in one hour.'

It is interesting that the Squadron Leader recalls that the Wellington 1C bombers of 26 OTU were newly built unlike his previous OTU which used operationally expired veteran aircraft. Indeed, the 26 OTU Wellingtons or at least those with the DV prefix had only been delivered from November of 1941 onwards from the Vickers Armstrong's factory in Chester.

In his book the Ralph Edwards does not mention his crew on that first raid. It was as follows:

P/O R.Edwards	Captain
W/O C.H.McKenzie	Navigator (Observer)
F/Sgt H.B.Davy	Wireless Operator
Sgt Woods	Front Gunner
F/Sgt W.E. Frew	Rear Gunner

The aircraft was Wellington 1C DV 908 Q.

The story continues,

> 'At eleven o'clock the aircraft began taking off in sequence. En route we were passed

by the huge dark shapes of the faster four engined Short Stirlings. We became concerned when we flew over a great deal of cloud out to sea, but the Met Officer had stated that the target area would be clear when we were due to arrive.'

The ORB report entitled 'Detail Of Work Carried Out' (which sounds very matter of fact considering the importance of the exercise), states that DV 908 took off from Graveley at 2324 hours and was actually the seventh of the 20 aircraft to depart. One can only imagine how the crew members felt at this stage of the operation especially those in action for the very first time. With the heart pumping and the adrenaline flowing they took their Wimpey on towards its target.

'At about 60 or 70 miles from Cologne the cloud banks suddenly cleared and we saw the ground beneath: a wonderful revelation under the steady floodlight effect of the brilliant moon. Ahead was a quite remarkable sight, a carpet of lurid fires and explosions around the target area such as we had never seen before. Numerous other aircraft were winging their way towards it and it was heartening to know that they were all on our side.'

The official report states that this aircraft bombed the target at 0130 hours at a height of 14000 feet. Squadron Leader Edwards recalls that moment,

'With the aid of fires and the broad stretch of the gleaming Rhine, we delivered our bomb load accurately and smoothly, the aircraft almost leaping upward with the sudden loss of weight. I peered down through the cockpit side window and saw the mushroom shaped explosion of our bombs amidst the fire and smoke that already swathed the city.'

Having dropped its bombs the Captain turned and headed back home but the return journey did not go quite to plan. Instead of returning to Graveley, they landed at Bourne in Lincolnshire,

'an easy error to make due to the fact that the outer airfield Drem lights were so close together.'

The flight had lasted five hours with the aircraft safely touching down at 0425. Just five minutes later, another 26 OTU Wellington, DV 780, crash landed at the same airfield, thankfully without injury to the crew.

On reflection the operation was considered a success and the large scale raids continued up to the end of June, with 26 OTU contributing further crews and aircraft.

The official report on the preparation, as it affected 26 OTU, no doubt assisted the organisation for the future raids. It begins by noting that the Unit was in fact given plenty of warning of its involvement in the raid,

'This Unit was advised of the 1000 Plan on the evening of the 21st May 1942, thus enabling considerable time to be spent on preparations and planning. In view of the recent opening of this OTU such a period of warning was badly needed.'

It was because Wing was a newly opened airfield and at that time not considered as class A, that it was deemed not ready to take on such an important operation. This explains the transfer of personnel and aircraft to Graveley although later raids did take off from Wing.

The report continues,

'Instructors had not been crewed up, and several recent arrivals were not too conversant with the Wellington aircraft, having operated on other types. Much equipment was needed and this was obtained from numerous sources. Lectures, checking of flying clothing and flying practices both day and night were carried out by instructors newly crewed up.'

This part of the report concludes by stating that,

'48 hours warning on future occasions would be enough, with perhaps two extra days for the maintenance of aircraft.'

When Squadron Leader Edwards suggests that the crews were keen to know what was being planned the report admits that,

'It is difficult to satisfy the curiosity of flying crews and ground crews, when all training suddenly ceases and every machine is made operationally serviceable.'

It then goes on to explain how they persuaded crews that the scheme was a Banquet exercise, with a warning to take practice seriously.

One of the difficulties evident from the report, was ensuring that all crews had enough flying kit, especially with twelve crews from 91 Group OTUs arriving to fly the spare aircraft. Of the 60 men involved only 19 arrived with full kit whilst five arrived with 'no kit of any description.' Not only were men arriving late without the full kit, but one Air Gunner and one Observer had not arrived at all by the 31st May, the day of the raid! It seems that these crews were reporting directly from leave and many had not given adequate details of the address at which they could be contacted.

With the force still assembled and with a low loss rate, the decision was made to mount a second raid, this time with Essen as the target, the very next night. 26 OTU contributed 15 aircraft with in most cases the same crews flying in the same aircraft. This was the situation for Ralph Edwards,

'The following night we performed – with great enthusiasm for a repeat success – a second intensive bombing raid. However, the meteorological conditions were not favourable, with a great deal of cloud on the route and over the target area and bombing accuracy was highly dubious. We returned home in a state of despondency and found other returned crews in similar mood.'

With the target obscured, the concentrated bombing as seen on the first raid was not repeated, although DV 908 officially dropped its bombload over the target area and returned safely, to Graveley this time, at 0337.

Sadly 26 OTU lost one more crew in Wellington HX 375. The following day the crews returned to their OTUs with many seeing action again soon after in their respective squadrons. The general feeling seemed to be that the use of OTUs in these operations not only ensured that enough aircraft were available, but also raised the morale of the participants whilst breaking the monotony of training routines. A further benefit was that crews would be posted to bomber squadrons with the experience of 'ops' behind them, whilst morale amongst instructors and groundcrews was also boosted by their involvement. On the other hand, there were some concerns. There were aircraft, for example, that were not modified to operational standards whilst pupils had not trained as crews and had been on standby over four nights. A further disadvantage was that armament and weapons were inadequate.

However, despite these concerns, OTUs continued to contribute to raids on German cities and 26 OTU was called upon again on the night of 25th June when the target was Bremen.

On this occasion 10 Wellingtons and crews were prepared and were joined by others from 13, 16 and 24 OTUs as part of the contribution of 92 Group. The raid was eventful with flak and fighter attacks reported by returning crews. One 26 OTU aircraft, DV 721, was lost with all crew members losing their lives.

This proved to be the last of the thousand bomber raids, although it was not the last occasion in which the Unit played a part in operations.

The increased defences of the German cities led to further training for pilots and crew in the form of Bullseyes, special air defence exercises that began in mid July over London by both day and night. As with other forms of training, these were not without accidents such as that which caused extensive damage to Wellington 1C, Z1389. The night of July 31st saw the resumption of bombing raids on German cities as part of Operation Grand National.

Dusseldorf was the target and the Unit contributed nine aircraft, all of which returned safely to Wing, despite higher concentrations of flak, searchlights and night fighters. These hazards were evident again during September raids on Dusseldorf, (with nine aircraft from the Unit), Bremen (twelve) and Essen (nine). During these, five aircraft were lost from 26 OTU and it was noticeable that the OTUs in general suffered most losses of the contributing force. This was of great concern as it deprived the Training units of experienced instructors who were not easy to replace and was in part responsible for the decision not to involve OTUs in large scale operations in the future.

It was to be almost a year before 26 OTU was involved in further bombing operations. These were part of Operation Starkey, which was mounted to test the basis of the D-Day plan, and required the Unit to contribute just four aircraft whose mission was to bomb ammunition dumps in the Foret d'Eperlecques in Northern France. For three, the raid was successful but for the fourth it proved fatal. Wellington X, HE 500,was reported missing, having crashed with no survivors at Rubrouck.

A further similar mission followed on the night of the 2nd September 1943, the 'special target' proving to be ammunition dumps in the Foret de Mormal. Two Wellington Mark 111 aircraft and one Wellington X were successful in bombing the target and returning unscathed to Wing.

The final operational mission from Wing occurred on the night of the 8th/9th September when four aircraft, including some of the crews from the previous raids, bombed another 'secret target', this time not named in the ORB. They were part of a 23 plane force from five OTUs and all succeeded in completing the task and returning safely.

During the operations listed above some 50+ aircrew lost their lives. What follows is a detailed account of the aircraft and crews that participated in these missions.

CHAPTER 9
The Aircraft and Crews Involved in Operations from 26 OTU

The following is a full list of aircraft and crews that took part in the various operations to which 26 OTU contributed. Because some aircraft and crews were involved in more than one operation, I have listed them in the order they appear in Appendix 1. Wherever possible I have added further information relating to the aircraft or crew members beyond their involvement in operations. Where omissions occur this is due to the information not existing on the original documents.

DV 719 R **Wellington 1C**

1. 30th/31st May 1942 – first 1000 Plan Raid – target Cologne. This aircraft took off at 2326 and bombed an area west of Hohenzollern Bridge at 0128, before returning at 0404.
   Crew:
   Sqdn Ldr A.A. Cookson – Captain
   P/O R.J. Emerson – Observer P/O F/Sgt P/O
   Cooper DFM – Wireless Operator
   Greaves – Front Gunner
   Corrie DFM – Rear Gunner

2. 1st/2nd June 1942 – second 1000 Plan Raid – target Essen. With the same crew on board, this aircraft took off at 2326 and successfully dropped its bomb load on the Krupps Works in Essen. It returned safely at 0402.

3. DV 719 had an eventful life, for after being involved in the above operations it suffered damage in an accident at Little Horwood on 11.9.42. Having been repaired, the aircraft was then involved in an amusing incident on 30.11.42. Sam Lawton picks up the story,

   'Something always happened when I was flying with my mate Jack Metcalf. In late November 1942, a Pupil Crew on a cross-country flight from Wing force landed at a very small Tiger Moth 'drome at Firbeck, near to Finningley, Yorkshire.... a miraculous landing! No pilot at Finningley would risk taking off on such a small 'drome which had only 500 yards of grass for a runway, a steep incline and was only being used by a Motor Transport Unit. Jack and I were sent to bring the Wimpy back. After spending the night in an old Nissen hut with the transport lads, we examined the aircraft and stripped it of all unessential equipment – guns,ammo,bed,Elsan, flares,oxygen bottles etc. Jack tested the engines and retained only 50 Gallons of fuel in each Nacelle Tank. After a slice of toast for breakfast Jack decided which was the best way to do a take-off run. He decided on – Rear turret in the hedge; down hill, down wind.... between the Colliery Dirt Tip and the Church steeple.

When the engines were started two interesting things happened.

First the Flight Lieutenant in charge of the Unit came and asked for our names, ranks and numbers, not at all concerned that we might be stealing the aircraft. Secondly, all the natives of the village, men, women and children in arms came to the gateway to see the end of their treasured historic sight.(The same women had been chasing the transport lads ever since they arrived!) Jack wanted me in the Second Pilot's seat for navigation. It was a misty morning, the engines were at full bore and we began to roll. Near the bottom of the field the wheels hit a concrete roadway, then the aircraft lifted and Jack immediately pulled hard on the control column. The machine lifted like a bird and both the church steeple and the dirt mound seemed merely feet away, to starboard and port respectively.'

After receiving guidance having sent an SOS, Jack and Sam landed safely at Finningley, but the Flying Control Officer refused to believe initially that theirs was the aircraft from Firbeck as they had forgotten to cancel the SOS. There was no need, however, for the machine to be disassembled and loaded on a Queen Mary to be driven back to Wing, as DV 719 was refuelled and flown back the same day by Jack Metcalf and Sam Lawton. It was undoubtedly some feat to get the Wimpy up in the air in such circumstances but Sam recalls ironically, that in the newspaper the very next day a story told of how a Flying Fortress took off on a runway of only 1000 yards!

4. The story of this aircraft ends with its demise in a crash on 2.3.44 after it had been passed on to 14 OTU.

DV 821 V **Wellington 1C**

1. 30th/31st May 1942 – first 1000 Plan Raid – target Cologne. This aircraft took off from Graveley at 2330 and dropped its bombs over the city at 0123 before returning safely at 0402.

   Crew:

   F/L R.P.Todd – Captain
   P/O F.C.Webb – Observer
   F/Sgt Watkins – Wireless Operator
   F/Sgt Moore – Front Gunner
   F/L J.Fenwick-Webb – Rear Gunner

2. The same crew were involved in the very next raid on the night of 1st/2nd June when Essen was bombed. They returned safely.

3. 13th/14th September 1942 – target Bremen.
   This aircraft returned to action being one of 12 from the Unit involved in this attack and one of three to have flown in the earlier raids. Having taken off from Wing at 2330 and bombing its target DV 821 returned home at 0540. On this occasion the crew was as follows:
   P/O V.H.Harris – Captain
   Sgt.D.C.Wilson – Observer
   Sgt.R.Bradbury – Wireless Operator
   P/O G.P.Kirwan – Front Gunner
   Sgt.A.A.Balcombe – Rear Gunner.

4. Wireless Operator, Sergeant Keightly was killed when this aircraft crash landed on bad ground at Greenhow Hill in Yorkshire after engine failure prevented it from maintaining height. This accident occurred just twelve days after the aircraft had flown in the raid on Bremen – 26.9.42.

DV 865 T **Wellington 1 C**

1. 30/31st May 1942 – first 1000 Plan raid – target Cologne. A successful mission saw this aircraft drop its bombs on target at 0120, having taken off at 2312. A safe return at 0408 was recorded.
   Crew:
   P/O C.J.Fooks – Captain
   W/O R.S.Bryant – Observer
   F/S W.R.Irving – Wireless Operator
   Sgt. C.L.Turner – Front Gunner
   Sgt. D.H.Baddeley – Rear Gunner

2. 1st/2nd June 1942 – target Essen.
   One of the 15 aircraft made ready to attack Essen but due to the starboard engine losing power and boost, DV 867 returned early without having reached its target. Take-off 2317, return 0031.

Crew as above.

3. With a new crew aboard, the aircraft was involved in the raid on Bremen on 25th/26th June. Take-off was at 2243 and the Dolmenherst area of the city was bombed before a safe return at 0420.
   Crew:
   Sgt I.B.McPherson – Captain
   F/S R.W.Pearson – Observer
   F/S K.G.Pollard – Wireless Operator
   Sgt K.J.Page – Front Gunner
   Sgt R.M.Fletcher – Rear Gunner

4. This aircraft saw further action when it was one of nine aircraft from 26 OTU to be selected for the raid on Dusseldorf on the night of 31st July 1942. On this occasion the aircraft took off from Wing. Another different crew were aboard, as follows:
   P/O Wilson – Captain
   F/S Watt – Observer
   Sgt Irving – Wireless Operator
   Sgt Page – Front Gunner
   Sgt Ferguson – Rear Gunner

Sergeants Page and Irving may have been the same crew members from the first two operational flights.

5. With another new crew aboard, this aircraft took off from Wing to attack Dusseldorf on the night of 10th September 1942. After take-off at 2056 no further news was received and the aircraft was reported missing.
   It later transpired that the aircraft crashed at 0032 near Weert in Holland with no survivors. The crew were buried at Venlo, but have since been moved to Jonkerbos War Cemetery. They were:
   Sgt A.I.L. Downs – Captain, Royal Australian Air Force
   Sgt J.J.Kearns – Observer
   Sgt R.U. Kirkpatrick – Wireless Operator
   Sgt J.W.Rowling – Front Gunner
   Sgt T.P.Allenby – Rear Gunner, Royal Canadian Air Force

DV 908 Q **Wellington 1C**

1. 30th/31st May 1942 – first 1000 Plan Raid – target Cologne. As already mentioned, this aircraft was flown by Ralph Edwards and his crew. A successful mission was recorded apart from the return flight which saw them land at Bourne, having been unable to locate Graveley. They were subsequently flown back to base and were ready for the next raid on Essen, the following day.

2. 1st/2nd June 1942 – target Essen. Generally regarded as a less than satisfactory raid, the crew at least had the consolation of knowing they dropped their bombs on target.
   Crew for both raids:
   P/O R.Edwards – Captain
   W/O C.H.McKenzie – Observer
   F/Sgt H.B Davey – Wireless Operator
   Sgt Woods – Front Gunner
   F/Sgt W.E. Frew – Rear Gunner

DV 823 Y **Wellington 1C**

1. 30th/31st May 1942 – first 1000 Plan Raid – target Cologne. A trouble free mission was recorded with the target being bombed at 0120, having taken off at 2322. Returned safely at 0350.
   Crew
   F/L P.T. Currie – Captain
   F/O P.C. Bargh – Observer
   Sgt.J.H. Austin – Wireless Operator
   F/Sgt P.G. Lyon – Front Gunner
   F/Sgt F.L. Calcutt – Rear Gunner

2. 1st/2nd June – target Essen.
   The same crew were aboard for the second 1000 Plan Raid. As with many others on this mission they reported low cloud which prevented accurate pin pointing although they were able to plot the main railway station at Duisburg and take photos at the time of bombing.

3. 25th/26th June – target Bremen.
   With a new crew, this aircraft was soon back in the action, being one of ten 26 OTU Wellingtons involved. A successful mission was reported with bombs being dropped on the south of the city.
   Crew:
   F/Sgt T.H. Bagnall – Captain
   F/Sgt G.E. Madgett – Observer
   Sgt P. Lavin – Wireless Operator
   Sgt J.W. Jennings – Front Gunner/2nd W/O
   F/Sgt A. C. Parker – Rear Gunner

4. 10th/11th September 1942 – target Dusseldorf. Excellent visibility enabled a successful bombing of the city with a safe return recorded. One of 9 aircraft to take-off from Wing. This crew, apart from the rear gunner, were to take part in two further raids in Wellington DV 941, but as can be seen under that entry the second of these was to prove fatal.
   Crew:
   Sgt L.W.Streeter – Captain Royal New Zealand Air Force.
   Sgt W.G.Archer –
   Sgt A.M.Bartlett –
   Sgt D.A.White –
   Sgt W.J.Landry –

5. The aircraft remained with 26 OTU until being moved on to 14 OTU where its life was ended in a crash landing on 3rd August 1943.

DV 780 Z **Wellington 1C**

1. 30th/31st May 1942 — first 1000 Plan Raid – target Cologne. Having taken off from Graveley at 2325, the bombing of the target was successfully completed before the aircraft turned for home. However, some difficulty in locating base, together with a shortage of fuel, saw the aircraft head for Bourne, where it crash landed, hitting the tail of a stationary aircraft. Fortunately the crew were uninjured and returned to base by road. Whilst flying over Cologne they reported spotting the cathedral illuminated by fire. After this traumatic landing, the crew were not required to take part in the following day's action. The aircraft itself was damaged beyond repair.
   Crew:
   P/O A.E. Allison – Captain
   P/O D.A. Templeton DFM – Observer
   Sgt R.S. Thompson – Wireless Operator
   Sgt H. Kay – Front Gunner
   Sgt N.D. Greenaway – Rear Gunner

DV 725 J **Wellington 1C**

1. 30th/31st May 1942 – first 1000 Plan Raid – target Cologne.
   A successful mission saw this aircraft drop its bomb load over the target area and return safely at 0505. Take off was at 2327.
   Crew.
   P/O W.A. McKay – Captain
   F/Sgt D.J McKendrie – Observer
   F/Sgt H. Savage – Wireless Operator
   Sgt S.T. Readmore – Front Gunner
   F/Sgt S.C. Matthews – Rear Gunner

For the second raid, the following night this crew flew a different aircraft for some reason not logged in records.

This was Wellington 1C DV 885 (see that entry).

2. Presumably there must have been some minor technical problem that caused this aircraft to remain on the ground during the raid on Essen on 1st/2nd June, however it was considered serviceable for the next raid – on Bremen – on 25th/26th June.
   Crew:
   P/O J.A. Wilson – Captain
   P/O D. Francis – Observer
   F/Sgt F.W. Christie – Wireless Operator
   F/Sgt J.H. Mahon – 2nd Wireless Operator
   Sgt A.E. Boorman – Rear Gunner

3. Action continued for DV 725 with a third foray over enemy territory as part of the force of nine 26 OTU aircraft involved in the attack on Dusseldorf on the night of 31st July/1st August 1942. Another new crew returned safely having successfully bombed the target at 0232.
   Crew:
   P/O Allison – Captain
   P/O Emmerson –
   Sgt Savage –
   Sgt Wood –
   F/Sgt Calcutt –

4. A fourth mission and a fourth crew for the raid on Bremen on 13th/14th September in which it was reported that the target was identified from observing the Weser River. Despite the pounding taken by the city both the Gothic city hall dating from the early 15th Century and the 11th Century Cathedral survived.
   Crew:
   Sgt A.W. Flack – Captain
   Sgt J. Shepherd –
   Sgt F.C. Detley –
   Sgt F.T. Boyd –
   Sgt H. Sponsler –

5. The final mission for this aircraft, one of only three to represent the Unit in five raids, was the attack on Essen on 16th/17th September 1942. It is reported that the primary bombs were abandoned due to overheating in the starboard engine but a safe return took place.
   Crew:
   Sgt D.C. Lowe – Captain
   Sgt P. Rogers –
   Sgt H.R. Jones –
   Sgt W. Shaw –
   Sgt W.R. Matthews –

6. Having completed operational flying the aircraft returned to training flights but was destroyed in a crash on 5th February 1943. The accident occurred over Cambridgeshire when, on realising they were unable to locate an airfield, the pilot, Sgt Beecher, took the decision to abandon the aircraft. The Unit report confirms that this was, in the circumstances, the correct decision.

DV 808 W **Wellington 1C**

1. 30th/31st May 1942 – first 1000 Plan Raid – target Cologne.
   This aircraft took off at 2314 and successfully dropped its bombs on the target area at 0128. The return journey caused some anxiety, as a suspicion of engine trouble forced the Captain to land at Manston. The crew were later flown back to Graveley.

2. The engine however, must have been given the all clear, for the aircraft with the same crew on board took part in the attack on Essen the very next night. Unfortunately the Captain made the decision to return early, before reaching the target, due to the starboard engine overheating. All bombs were brought back as a result.
   The crew on each occasion was:
   F/Sgt H. Lewis – Captain
   F/Sgt H. McLeod – Observer
   F/Sgt I. Hoy – Wireless Operator
   Sgt F. Ball – Front Gunner
   Sgt J. Lamb – Rear Gunner

3. After service with 26 OTU the aircraft passed firstly to 11 then 21 OTU before suffering damage on 18.12.43. which brought an end to its flying days.

DV 825 U **Wellington 1C**

1. 30/31st May – first 1000 Plan Raid – target Cologne.
   After take-off at 2341, this aircraft completed a successful mission, bombing the west side of the city at 0150 before returning safely to Graveley at 0513.

2. With the same crew on board, the aircraft saw action the next night when it attacked Essen. Despite the general disappointment with this attack, this aircraft did drop its bombs on the target area returning at 0443.
   Crew for both missions:
   F/Sgt G. Morley – Captain
   Sgt H. Jordan – Observer
   F/Sgt Whitham – Wireless Operator
   F/Sgt L. Beck – Front Gunner
   F/Sgt A. Parker – Rear Gunner

3. With a new crew on board, this aircraft was involved on the raid on Bremen on the 25/26th June 1942. Although take-off was recorded at 2237, the aircraft was forced to abandon its bombs over the Dutch Coast and return to base owing to Wireless Telegraphy problems.
   Crew:
   P/O W.G.K. Gorrie – Captain
   P/O H. Cobb DFM – Observer
   F/Sgt R. White – First Wireless Operator
   Sgt G. Hearn – Second Wireless Operator
   Sgt K. Blackhurst – Rear Gunner

Pilot Officer Gorrie, later Squadron Leader, was in command of C Flight at one stage in his career at Wing and was at the Unit for a considerable time.

4. The end for this aircraft came in an accident at Cheddington on 30th August 1942. (See Appendix 2)

DV 723 H **Wellington 1C**

1. 30th/31st May 1942 – first 1000 Plan Raid – target Cologne.
This mission was the first of six that this aircraft was involved in, which makes it the most used of all 26 OTU aircraft as far as operations are concerned. Sadly, however, the final mission was to be fatal for both the aircraft and its crew. On this first raid all went well with departure from Graveley at 2335 and a safe return recorded at 0436.
Crew:
P/O Wilson – Captain
P/O D. Francis – Observer
F/Sgt Pollard – Wireless Operator
F/Sgt Christie DFM – Front Gunner
Sgt A.E. Borman – Rear Gunner

2. The same crew minus F/Sqt Pollard later flew in DV725 on raids over Bremen. (see that entry for details). They were required to crew this aircraft, however, for the raid on Essen the next night. Again no problems were reported and bombs were dropped on the target area at 0108 before a safe return at 0406.

3. 31st July/1st August 1942 – attack on Dusseldorf.
Another trouble free mission was reported by the new crew, one of just nine required from the Unit. Take off from Wing was at 0021 with the return at 0443.
Crew:
P/O Taylor – Captain
P/O Garside –
Sgt Potter –
Sgt Garbutt –
F/Sgt Higham –

It is interesting to note that the maximum number of operations for any aircraft from the Unit during 1942 was seven and that for reasons unknown this particular aircraft did not participate in the third of these, the raid on Bremen on 25th/26th June.

4. Another new crew boarded DV 723 for the raid on Dusseldorf on the night of 10th/11th September but they were unable to complete the mission as the aircraft would not climb above 9300 feet. Being forced to turn for home they arrived without mishap at 2305.
Crew:
P/O V.H. Harris – Captain
Sgt D.C. Wilson –

Sgt R. Bradbury –
P/O G.P. Kirwan –
Sgt A.A. Balcombe –

5. Despite the problems encountered just three days earlier the aircraft was again wheeled out for the attack on Bremen on the night of 13th/14th September.
Whether the Unit found it difficult to find the twelve aircraft it was asked to provide or whether it was felt that any problems with the aircraft were considered rectified I am unable to determine but, as it was, DV 723 was called into action. Take-off was recorded at 2345 but again difficulties were encountered when the starboard engine caught fire. The captain jettisoned the cowling in the sea off Tisiel and they returned to Wing safely at 0344. This must have been a worrying time for the crew and one cannot but think they must have been a little concerned when they were informed that in just two days time they would be flying on another raid in the same aircraft.

6. Their fears sadly were justified for soon after take-off at 2019 on 16th September 1942 bound for Essen they were reported missing. No trace of the crew or aircraft was discovered and the brave fliers are commemorated on the Runnymede Memorial.
The crew for this and the above mission was:
Sgt P.L. Looney – Captain – Royal Australian Air Force.
Sgt M.J. Clayton –
Sgt J.T. Pate –
Sgt A.E.W. Butler –
Sgt C.G. Calcutt –

DV 707 D **Wellington 1C**

1. 30th/31st May 1942 – first 1000 Plan Raid – target Cologne.
This recently arrived aircraft was reported missing after take-off from Graveley at 2315. It was later discovered that it had been shot down by a night fighter and crashed near Venlo in Holland where all but one of the crew were at first buried. The one survivor, Wireless Operator Flight Sergeant D.W.Caswell, was captured and taken, severely wounded, to Stalag Luft Sagan and Belaria. Flight Sergeant Ford and Flight Sergeant Barker had previously flown with 9 Squadron and 103 Squadron respectively. With those of their fellow crew members their bodies were taken to Jonkerbos War Cemetery in 1945.
Crew.
F/Sgt E.J. Ford DFM – Captain
F/O D.C. August – Observer
F/Sgt D.W. Caswell – Wireless Operator
F/Sgt J. Thompson – Front Gunner
F/Sgt F.F. Barker DFM – Rear Gunner

DV 871 P **Wellington 1C**

1. 30th/31st May 1942 – first 1000 Plan Raid – target Cologne.
   One of the twenty 26 OTU aircraft to take-off from Graveley on this first 1000 bomber raid. Take-off was at 2339 and bombs were dropped on the centre of Cologne at 0144, but due to slight engine trouble the Captain was forced to land at Waterbeach airfield from where he and his crew were driven back to Graveley. Although the aircraft was from 26 OTU the crew were members of 22 OTU.
   Crew:
   P/O Jackson – Captain
   Sgt Smith – Observer
   Sgt A.G. Daniels – Wireless Operator
   Sgt Freysteinson
   (Freinsteinson) – Bombardier
   Sgt Dempsey – Air Gunner

Note: The official Unit documents detailing crew involved use the terms Bombardier and Air Gunner for crew members from 22 and 27 OTU whilst Front and Rear Gunners are used for 26 OTU crewmen.

2. The same crew were aboard for the following day's raid on Essen suggesting that the aircraft was returned to Graveley in serviceable condition. Perhaps there was some apprehension about this within the crew, although at such times there was probably already enough anxiety about the mission ahead of them. As for most aircraft on this raid the pin pointing of the target was difficult due to the cloud cover, officially documented in the ORB as 5 to 8/10 stratus cloud at 5/8000 feet. However, the raid was completed and the aircraft returned safely at 0345.

3. 31st July/1st August – target Dusseldorf.
   This aircraft was one of the nine from the Unit used on raid and completed the task with no problems reported. Crew on this occasion were also from 26 OTU. They took off from Wing at 0028 and returned at 0543.
   Crew:
   F/Sgt T.H.Bagnall – Captain
   F/Sgt G.E.Madgett –
   Sgt Goff –
   Sgt Jennings –
   F/Sgt Allen –

4. 10th/11th September – target Dusseldorf.
   The first two named crew members from the above raid returned to Dusseldorf with this

aircraft along with three new colleagues. They took off from Wing at 2037 and bombed the aerodrome at Hamstede at 2227 but were forced to return early as they were unable to climb above 7500 feet. Their safe return is recorded at 0005.

Crew:

F/Sgt T.H. Bagnall	– Captain
F/Sgt G.E. Madgett	–
F/Sgt S. Hird	–
Sgt. A.Simpson	–
F/Sgt R.Young	–

5. Having survived operational duties this aircraft continued its role as a training bomber with 26 OTU before seeing service with 21,15 and 28 OTUs. It was finally Struck Off Charge on 30th March 1944.

HX 375 X **Wellington 1C**

1. 30th/31st May 1942 – first 1000 Plan Raid – target Cologne.
   This aircraft was possibly not as new as those with the DV prefix, but successfully completed its first operational duty with the Unit, dropping its bombs over the target at 0110 and returning safely to Graveley at 0355. The crew members were from 22 OTU and were as follows:

Sgt Edmunds	– Captain
Sgt Utman (Upmand)	– Observer – Royal Canadian Air Force
Sgt Horner	– Wireless Operator/Air Gunner
Sgt Edye – Bombardier	– Royal Australian Air Force
Sgt Lenihek (Lenchek)	– Air Gunner

There appears some confusion as to the correct spellings of two of the crews surnames as both are found in the Unit documents.

2. As with the majority of aircraft and crew involved in the above raid, the next night saw them in action again in the attack on Essen. However after take-off at 2259 the aircraft was reported missing. The crew were finally buried in Schooselof Cemetery, Antwerp. There remains some doubt about the make up of the crew as in his book on World War II RAF Losses (Volume 3), author W.R Chorley names the Air Gunner as F/Sgt R.I.Derry of the Royal Canadian Air Force. Apparently the cousin of Sgt Edye was killed in April whilst serving with 27 OTU.

DV 709 F **Wellington 1C**

1. 30th/31st May 1942 – first 1000 Plan Raid – target Cologne.
   This proved to be the only operation for this aircraft and a tragic one at that, for although

the target was successfully bombed, the aircraft crashed near the flour mill at Soham on its return whilst attempting an emergency landing. The ORB report states that four of the crew lost their lives, whilst W.R.Chorley states that two died and four were injured and taken to the RAF Hospital at Ely. Whether two of the injured died whilst there is not clear, however it is certain that the Captain and Air Gunner were killed.

Crew:

Sgt J.J. Dixon – Captain
Sgt Scroggie – Observer – Royal Canadian Air Force
Sgt Broadhurst – Wireless Operator
Sgt Green – Bombardier
Sgt B.B. Camlin – Air Gunner

The crew who were probably not from 26 OTU were waiting to join 57 Squadron at the time.

DV 868 E **Wellington 1C**

1. 30th/31st May 1942 – first 1000 Plan Raid – target Cologne.
   This aircraft took off from Graveley at 2332 and bombed north of the main fires over Cologne, on the west side of the Rhine at 0150. Despite receiving damage to the electrical system from flak, the aircraft made a safe return at 0446.
   Crew, from 22 OTU:
   P/O Stickell – Captain
   P/O Robertson – Observer
   Sgt O'Neill – Wireless Operator/Air Gunner
   Sgt Wilson – Bombardier
   Sgt Beale – Air Gunner

2. The damage sustained in the above raid was presumably, serious enough to mean that the aircraft was not operational for the following night's raid on Essen, however there was no respite for the crew who were given another aircraft (DV 915 – see entry). DV 868 returned to action on 31st July for the attack on Dusseldorf, but further bad fortune meant it had to return early having not dropped its bombs.
   Crew:
   Sgt Gill – Captain
   Sgt Appi –
   Sgt Minchin –
   F/Sgt Hird –
   F/Sgt Lancaster –

3. The aircraft returned to training use after this but was soon after destroyed in an accident at Cheddington, where it crashed attempting to overshoot the runway. (see Accidents Appendix 2). The date of this being 12th August 1942.

DV 703 B **Wellington 1C**

1. 30th/31st May 1942 – first 1000 Plan Raid – target Cologne.
   Crewed by members of 27 OTU this aircraft dropped its bombs on the west side of the Rhine before returning at 0502. Take off is recorded as 2359.
   Crew:
   Sgt Foderingham – Captain
   Sgt Gordon – Observer
   Sgt Stewart – Wireless Operator
   Sgt Cobbett – Bombardier
   Sgt Sutherland – Air Gunner

2. The same crew were aboard for the raid on Essen the next night. All went smoothly with a safe return at 0435.

3. The aircraft was not utilised again until the raid on Dusseldorf on the night of 10th September. Take off was recorded as 2056 but the aircraft was not heard of again, being reported missing. All but one of the crew perished and are buried in the Rheinberg War Cemetery. The survivor, Sgt Hedley, was taken to Stalag Lamsdorf.
   Crew:
   Sgt C.C. Ogilvie – Captain – Royal Australian Air Force
   Sgt L. Hedley –
   Sgt J. McIveen –
   Sgt J.W. Gardner –
   Sgt J.B. Higginson – Royal Canadian Air Force

W 5704 S **Wellington 1C**

1. 30th/31st May 1942 – first 1000 Plan Raid – target Cologne.
   Tragedy again struck the Unit as this aircraft was shot down by a night fighter as it flew over Holland. It crashed at Middlebeers, 16km west of Eindhoven with no survivors. They are laid to rest at the Woensel General Cemetery. The crew members who were likely to have been from 27 OTU were:
   F/O Whiting – Captain
   Sgt Garrick – Observer
   Sgt Young – Wireless Operator – Royal New Zealand Air Force
   Sgt Hall – Bombardier – Royal New Zealand Air Force
   Sgt Williams – Air Gunner

DV 710 G **Wellington 1C**

1. 30th/31st May 1942 – first 1000 Plan Raid – target Cologne.

In the ORB documents this aircraft is recorded as DV 701, although in the next raid the above number is given and research indicates that DV 701 was not attached to the Unit. The Captain reported that they could not see their own bombs drop over the target due to the large number of fires. A safe return saw the aircraft land at 0420. The crew were from 27 OTU:

Sgt Keats – Captain
Sgt Hetherington – Observer
Sgt Williams – Wireless Operator
Sgt Spence – Bombardier
Sgt Miller – Air Gunner

2. The crew reassembled the next night for the Essen raid and completed the mission safely.

3. Two weeks after the above raid, on the 14th June, the aircraft was destroyed in a training accident at Cheddington whilst landing. (See accidents – Appendix 2)

DV 740 O **Wellington 1C**

1. 30th/31st May 1942 – first 1000 Plan Raid – target Cologne.
Another tragic story relates to this aircraft which, although the first of the Unit's aircraft to be airborne on this raid, was soon to be reported missing. Take off was recorded as 2305 but over Holland it was shot down by a night fighter and crashed at Alem near Oss. Sgt Hillyer survived and was taken to Stalag Luft Heydekrug but sadly the rest of the crew lost their lives and are buried in Uden War Cemetery.
Crew:
Sgt F.G. Hillyer – Captain
Sgt D.H. Fletcher – Observer
Sgt D.S. Vincent – Wireless Operator
P/O A.C.White – Bombardier
Sgt H.C.Smith – Air Gunner

DV 721 H **Wellington 1C**

1. 30th/31st May 1942 – first 1000 Plan Raid – target Cologne.
This aircraft took off from Graveley at 2328 and bombed the south of Cologne west of the Rhine before returning to Oakington airfield for reasons not known. The crew from 27 OTU were:
Sgt Isaacson – Captain
Sgt Gardiner – Observer
Sgt Pepper – Wireless Operator
Sgt Sedgley – Bombardier
Sgt Anivitti – Air Gunner

2. The same crew set off the next night to attack Essen, but again landed at a different airfield,

Bourne on this occasion. The target area was identified only by the glare of fires under the cloud cover.

3. On its third operational flight, to attack Bremen on 25th June this aircraft and its new crew were lost. They are buried in Kiel War Cemetery.
   F/Sgt Stirling DFM – Captain – Royal New Zealand Air Force
   F/Sgt Jordan –
   F/Sgt Watkins –
   F/O Sharples –
   F/Sgt Baddeley –

The Captain had previously served for 150 Squadron with whom he was awarded the Distinguished Flying Medal. F/O Sharples at 43 was considerably older than the rest of the crew and well above the average age of aircrew in general.

DV 885 A **Wellington 1C**

1. 1st/2nd June 1942 Second 1000 Plan Raid – target Essen.
   This aircraft was brought as a replacement for aircraft lost in the previous night's raid on Cologne, but having reached the Dutch Coast returned early due to problems with the engine throttle controls and rear turret intercom.
   Crew:
   P/O McKay – Captain
   F/Sgt McKendry –
   F/Sgt Savage –
   Sgt Beardmore –
   F/Sgt Matthews –

This crew had flown the previous night in DV 725 and Cpt McKay, F/Sgt Savage and F/Sgt Matthews were also involved in the raid on Bremen on 25th/26th June in DV 896.

2. 31st July/1st August 1942 – raid on Dusseldorf.
   A new crew were allocated for this attack which went smoothly with bombs being dropped on target. The aircraft returned at 0524 having taken off at 0025.
   Crew:
   P/O W.G.K. Gorrie – Captain
   Sgt Hunter – Observer
   F/Sgt R.C.White – Wireless Operator
   Sgt G. Hearn – 2nd Wireless Operator
   Sgt K.R. Blackhurst – Rear Gunner

Apart from the Observer, this crew had flown in DV 825 in the attack on Bremen on 25th June.

3. Called into action again on 10th September being one of the nine aircraft from the Unit to be involved in the attack on Dusseldorf on that night. However problems occurred when the Starboard throttle control became disconnected and the Captain turned for home. Its bombs were dropped in the sea before a safe return was made. This particular raid proved to be something of a disaster for the Unit as two aircraft were lost and five returned early leaving only two who made a trouble free run.

   Crew:
   Sgt R.J. Carson – Captain
   Sgt C.A.Smith –
   Sgt F.Sayles –
   P/O J.C.Cogill –
   Sgt R.J.Booth –

This crew were to fly in DV 822 in the attack on Bremen on the night of 13th September.

4. Another new crew were involved for the attack on Bremen mentioned above.The captain reported haze and smoke up to 5000ft but no cloud. Despite receiving some damage from a fighter the aircraft returned safely having bombed an area in the vicinity of the Deschimag Works. The crew were to fly in R1224 in the attack on Essen on 16th September but were unable to take off.

   They were:
   Sgt G.K. Easter – Captain
   Sgt J.B. Williams –
   Sgt J. Banyer –
   Sgt L.H. Pattisson –
   Sgt N.R. Hutchins –

Having returned to training duty following these operations this aircraft was to be lost to the Unit in an accident at Little Horwood on 6th November. (Details in Appendix 2).

DV 915 E **Wellington 1C**

1. 1st/2nd June 1942 – attack on Essen.
   The aircraft took off at 2304 with a crew from 22 OTU but was attacked by a fighter over Essen sustaining damage to the hydraulics together with a broken air bottle. Bombs were dropped, however, before the Captain turned for home. He decided not to make for Wing and instead made a good landing at West Malling despite overrunning the runway.

   Crew:
   P/O Stickle – Captain
   P/O Robertson –
   Sgt O'Neil –
   Sgt Wilson –
   Sgt Beale –

2. 10th/11th September 1942 – attack on Dusseldorf.
   Presumably having suffered minor damage during the above raid certain repair work was necessary and this may have prevented the aircraft from being considered for use in the two raids in late June and July.
   By September, however, the aircraft was ready for action and a crew from 26 OTU climbed aboard destined for Dusseldorf. They would undoubtedly have been disappointed when it became apparent that all was not well as they were unable to climb above 8000 feet. The decision was made to return to base and in order to lighten the load two bombs were jettisoned, before the remainder were dropped in the sea. A safe return was made.
   Crew:
   S/L L.P. Massey – Captain
   P/O D.A. Templeton –
   Sgt J.W. Minchin –
   Sgt K.J. Page –
   Sgt W.C. Ferguson –

3. The aircraft was again utilised for the raid on Bremen just two nights later and bombs were dropped on the target before being attacked by a Junkers 88. The rear gunner replied without hitting the enemy aircraft and with only slight damage sustained a safe return was made.
   Crew:
   Sgt F.L. Welford – Captain
   Sgt S.N. Marsh –
   Sgt J.H. Griffiths –
   Sat E.P. Coyle –

This crew apart from Sgt Scanlon were to fly in DV 732 in the raid on Essen on the night of 16th/17th September.

4. Another new crew were aboard when this aircraft was again called into action for the attack on Essen mentioned above. For once this proved a trouble free operation for DV 915 with bombs being dropped in the target area despite slight ground haze and much smoke obscuring vision.
   Crew:
   Sgt R.M.Kidd – Captain
   Sgt R.W.Lewis –
   Sgt E.Bell –
   Sgt J.S.Reed –
   Sgt R.L.Beattie –

This crew had previously been aboard DV 846 in the previous raid and in DV 941 on the Dusseldorf operation. On neither of these were they able to reach the target so some satisfaction must have been gained on this occasion.

5. Having survived four operations over enemy territory this aircraft was destroyed in an horrific accident over Hogshaw bomb range when it collided with another Wellington Z8950. (Full details in Appendix 2).

DV 896 D Wellington 1C

1. 25th/26th June – attack on Bremen.
   Despite noticeable flak and general aircraft activity in the target area, bombs were dropped on what was thought to be Oldenburg, before a safe return was made.
   Crew:
   P/O W.A. McKay – Captain
   P/O D.A.Templeman DFO –Observer
   F/S M.Savage – Wireless Operator
   Sgt H.Kay – 2nd Wireless Operator
   F/S S.C.Matthews – Rear Gunner

The Captain and Observer flew together in later operations in DV 846 and DV 714 .

2. The aircraft was not required again for bombing operations until the attack on Essen on 16th/17th September 1942 but on this occasion the Captain was forced to return early as the aircraft would not climb above 8500 feet. The crew, which had been aboard DV 725 on the previous raid on Bremen were:
   Sgt A.W. Flack – Captain
   Sgt J. Shepherd –
   Sgt F.C. Detley –
   Sgt F.T. Bond (Boyd) –
   Sgt H. Sponsler –

3. No further bombing operations were undertaken with the aircraft continuing its training role before being passed on to 21 OTU and later 15 OTU before being struck off charge on 31.3.1946.

Z 8841 S Wellington 1C

1. 25th/26th June 1942 – attack on Bremen.
   The aircrafts only involvement in a bombing operation with 26 OTU proved successful with bombs being dropped on target and a safe return recorded. The Captain reported "red glows under cloud".
   Crew:
   W/O G.A. Morley – Captain
   W/O R.C. Bryant – Observer

F/S J.W. Minchin – Wireless Operator
Sgt S.P. Wood – 2nd Wireless Operator
F/S R. Lancaster – Rear Gunner

This was the Captain's third operational flight with the Unit, having piloted DV 825 in previous raids.

X 9823 X **Wellington 1C**

1. 25th/26th June 1942 – attack on Bremen.
   In its first operational flight with the Unit this aircraft was forced to return early with bombs intact due to problems with the artificial horizon.
   Crew:
   P/O W.R. Suggitt – Captain
   F/S J. Watt – Observer
   F/S I.B. Hoy – Wireless Operator
   Sgt P.G. Lyon – 2nd Wireless Operator
   P/O J.E. Lamb – Rear Gunner

2. Dusseldorf on the 31st July/1st August was the only other bombing operation with the Unit. This proved trouble free with the target being bombed and a safe return reported. The aircraft was again piloted by P/O Suggitt but with a new crew:
   W/O McKenzie –
   F/S Christie –
   F/S McMahon –
   Sgt Fletcher –

DV 801 F **Wellington 1C**

1. 25th/26th June 1942 – attack on Bremen.
   This proved to be the only bombing raid undertaken by this aircraft whilst with 26 OTU. It proved to be eventful but thankfully both crew and aircraft returned in one piece. Having taken off from Wing at 2245 they were attacked by a Junkers 88 before the target area was reached. The Captain decided to jettison the bombs at this stage, whilst the rear gunner claimed a possible hit on the attacker. On returning to Wing a skillful belly landing was performed because of damage to the hydraulic system.
   Crew:
   P/O F.V. Taylor – Captain
   F/O E. Garside – Observer
   Sgt A.E. Elphick – Wireless Operator
   Sgt W. Friend – 2nd Wireless Operator
   P/O M. Corrie DFM – Rear Gunner.

2. The aircraft continued with the Unit before seeing service with 6 OTU and 3 OTU before finally being struck off charge on 28.1.44.

DV 774 A **Wellington 1C**

1. 25th/26th June 1942 – attack on Bremen.
   This proved to be the aircraft's only bombing raid although trouble was encountered when the Distributor was discovered being set at "safe" which prevented any bombs being dropped.
   Crew:
   F/Sgt N.V. Gill – Captain
   F/Sgt W. Airs – Observer
   Sgt S.J. Goff – Wireless Operator
   F/Sgt S. Hird – 2nd Wireless Operator
   Sgt Dawson – Rear Gunner.

DV 941 **Wellington 1C**

1. 31st July/1st August 1942 – attack on Dusseldorf.
   A successful bombing of the target area, more specifically Nevso, having taken off from Wing at 0001. A safe return was made at 0403.
   Crew
   P/O Bowyer – Captain
   F/Sgt Pearson –
   Sgt Lavin –
   Sgt Simpson –
   P/O Stephen-Smith. –

2. The aircraft was utilised for a return visit to Dusseldorf on the 10th/11th September, but on this occasion the Captain was forced to return early as the aircraft would not climb above 9300 feet.
   Crew:
   Sgt R.M.Kidd – Captain
   Sgt R.W.Lewis –
   Sgt F.Bell –
   Sgt J.S.Reed –
   Sgt R.L.Beattie –

This crew were due to take part in the Bremen raid on the night of 13th/14th September in DV846, but failed to take off. (see entry for DV846).

3. In that same raid on Bremen this aircraft successfully dropped its bombs on the Atlas Works and nearby docks aided no doubt by ' good visibility' as reported by the Captain.

Crew:
Sgt L.W. Streeter RNZAF – Captain
Sgt W.G.Archer –
Sgt A.McK.Bartlett –
Sgt D.A.White RCAF –

4. The same crew were aboard for the next raid on Essen but it ended in tragedy for the aircraft crashed into the sea off the Dutch coast with no survivors. The Captain is buried in the Noordwijk Cemetery, whilst Sgt Johnson is buried in the New Amsterdam Cemetery. The remaining members of the crew have no known graves. Sergeant Lawrie Streeter enlisted with the Royal New Zealand Air Force in 1941 after gaining his 'wings' in his homeland. He left for England in January 1942 and his flying-log indicates training at BAT Flight Middleton and No.15 AFU Leconfield in Yorkshire, before joining 26 OTU in July, initially at Cheddington.
In the College Journal of his Otahuhu High School an obituary was written in which Lawrie Streeter is described as, 'a likeable lad who won the esteem of pupils and teachers alike for his integrity of character. He was a keen member of the School Bible Class and took an interest in all sport.'

DV 846 O **Wellington 1C**

1. Dusseldorf raid 31st July/1st August 1942.
On its first mission with 26 OTU the aircraft suffered engine trouble leaving the Captain with little alternative other than to return to Wing with bombs intact.
Crew:
P/O W.A. McKay – Captain
P/O D.A. Templeton DFM –
Sgt I.B. Hoy –
Sgt P.G. Lyon –
F/O Collard –

The first two named had previously flown on the Bremen raid of 25th June, whilst the two Sergeants had also taken part in the Bremen raid in X9823.

2. The aircraft again failed to reach its destination when utilised for the next raid on Bremen on the night of 13th/14th September 1942. On this occasion it failed to leave the ground due to surging in one engine. This must have been particularly frustrating for the crew who had already suffered the disappointment of failing to reach the target when they flew in DV 941 for the attack on Dusseldorf on 10th/11th September.
They were:
Sgt R.M. Kidd – Captain
Sgt R.W. Lewis –
Sgt E. Bell –

Sgt J.S. Reed –
Sgt R.L. Beattie –

3. This aircraft was eventually passed on to 28 OTU before being struck off charge on 28.1.44.

DV 732 H Wellington 1C

1. The crew for this raid on Dusseldorf on 10th/11th September were embarking on the first of three operational flights with 26 OTU, the last of which was to prove fatal with all members losing their lives. (For details see DV723). This raid, however, was completed with no problems, the target being bombed from 10,400 feet followed by a safe return.
   Crew:
   Sgt P.L. Looney – Captain – Royal Australian Air Force.
   Sgt M.J. Clayton –
   Sgt J.T. Pate –
   Sgt A.E.W. Butler –
   Sgt C.G. Calcutt –

2. For the raid on Essen on 16th/17th September 1942 the aircraft was flown by Sgt F.L.Welford and his crew who had been in DV915 for the previous raid on Bremen on 13th/14th September. On this occasion though they were forced to abandon their task south of Cambridge due to problems with the rear turret intercom.
   Crew
   Sgt F.L. Welford – Captain
   Sgt S.N. Marsh –
   Sgt J.H. Griffiths –
   Sgt E.P. Coyle –
   Sgt H.I. Stott – he in fact was not a member of the crew in DV 915.

3. The aircraft was not considered for further use in bombing raids and was passed to 11 OTU where it was destroyed in a crash on 2nd June 1943.

DV 822 Y Wellington 1C

1. The only occasion when this aircraft was required for bombing operations was for the raid on Bremen of 13/14th September 1942. The Captain reported that the target was bombed at 0216 with the glow of the fires visible. However the aircraft was hit by flak which punctured the starboard wheel and this caused it to swerve off the runway on landing. Thankfully no injuries were sustained and no further damage to the aircraft. The crew had previously flown in DV 885 on the raid on Dusseldorf of 10th/11th September.

They were:

Sgt R.J. Carson	–	Captain
Sgt C.A. Smith	–	
Sgt F. Sayles	–	
P/O J.C. Cogill	–	
Sgt R.J. Booth	–	

DV 714 Wellington 1C

1. This aircraft took part in the raid on Bremen of 13th/14th September 1942. Departing at 0001 a trouble free mission was recorded which saw the target bombed at 0245 with a safe return at 0550.
   Crew:
   Sgt B.P. Shaddick – Captain
   Sgt E. Watcham
   Sgt F.B. Hough
   Sqt E.C. Woollard
   Sgt G.A. Fitzgerald

2. A new crew took over for the raid on Essen of 16th/17th September. Again a straightforward mission was accomplished with bombs being dropped over Essen in a slight haze.
   Crew:

P/O C.C.J. Bowyer	–	Captain
P/O D.A. Templeton	–	(see DV846)
P/O F.V. Taylor	–	
Sgt G.A. Potter	–	
Sgt G. Walker	–	

3. The aircraft was later damaged beyond repair after it had been passed to 28 OTU.

X9786 – Wellington 1C

1. At 23.53 on the night of 13th September 1942 this aircraft took off from Wing bound for Bremen along with eleven other Wellingtons of 26 OTU. Whether it reached the target and dropped its bombs is not known, but what has emerged is that it was shot down by a night fighter piloted by Hptm Wilhelm Dormann and crashed into the Ijsselmeer lake in the Netherlands at 0548. One crew member, Sergeant Gartlan, survived and was taken to Stalag Lamsdorf as a prisoner of war. The remainder of the crew perished and are buried in the New Eastern Cemetery, Amsterdam.
   Crew:

P/O R.L. Hage	–
Sgt A.K. Smith	–

Sgt K.D.J ones –
Sgt D. Fisher –
Sgt J.A. Gartlan – Royal Canadian Air Force.

R1224 **Wellington 1C**

1. 13th/14th September 1942 – attack on Bremen.
   This aircraft took off from Wing at 2341 and returned safely at 0554 having bombed the target area. The Captain reported 'no cloud but hazy. River and many fires seen'. The crew who were to fly in DV725 in the raid on Essen just three days later were:
   Sgt D.C. Lowe – Captain
   Sgt P. Rogers –
   Sgt H.R. Jones –
   Sgt W. Shaw –
   Sgt W.R. Matthews –

2. Although required for the Essen attack the aircraft failed to take off due to fluctuating engine revs. The crew had previously flown in DV 885 in the Bremen raid and consisted of:
   Sgt G.K. Easter – Captain
   Sgt J.B.T. Williams –
   Sgt J. Banyer –
   Sgt L.H. Pattison –
   Sgt N.R. Hutchins –

3. For more details of this aircraft's service see the Chapter entitled 'On The Ground'.

DV844 **Wellington 1C**

1. 13th/14th September 1942 – attack on Bremen.
   This was the only bombing raid the aircraft was involved in whilst at 26 OTU and it proved to be unsuccessful as the Captain was forced to return early with all bombs intact. The reason for this course of action was a shortage of oxygen with it being reported that the supply was nearly expended halfway to the Dutch coast.
   Crew:
   Sgt J.R. Rodgers – Captain
   Sgt F.L.A. Morris –
   Sgt Y. Lewis –
   Sgt A.J. Johnson –
   Sgt J.A. Sneddon –

2. The aircraft was not required for the Essen raid that followed but the crew were and flew in replacement Wellington DV697.

3. Formerly with 25 OTU DV 844 was to move on to 15,21 and 85 OTU before being struck off charge on 8th November 1946.

DV697 **Wellington 1C**

1. 16th/17th September 1942 – attack on Essen.
   It is possible that this aircraft was utilised as replacement for DV 844 which had been dogged with problems on the previous raid. The crew were the same although they fared only slightly better on this occasion with the aircraft failing to climb above 10,000ft. However they were able to report that bombs were dropped on an aerodrome in the target area. The raid itself was most unsatisfactory as far as 26 OTU was concerned as of the nine aircraft that were involved only two managed a trouble free run.
   Crew:
   Sgt J.R. Rodgers – Captain
   Sgt F.L.A. Morris –
   Sgt Y. Lewis –
   Sgt A.J. Johnson –
   Sgt J.A. Sneddon –

2. This aircraft which had previously flown with 103 Squadron moved on to 14 OTU but was damaged beyond repair in a heavy landing at Market Harborough.

CHAPTER 10
Other Forms of Operational Flying

Besides the bombing raids there were other occasions when aircraft and crews were required to take part in operations of one sort or another. One form of these was code named Nickel and involved the dropping of leaflets, mainly over towns along or near the French coast. The first of these took place in May 1943 and involved just three aircraft, but they were soon to be a regular feature of the Unit, with six such sorties being recorded for July of the same year. The practice was obviously extended for, during the last three months of the year, some twenty-six Nickel sorties were recorded. As with most other flying operations, incidents and accidents occurred. The first recorded in the ORB was not serious, requiring Wellington X3403 to land at RAF Warmwell on just one engine. It had been one of four aircraft that had dropped leaflets over Alencon, Le Mans, Argentan and Laval. Bruce Giles recalls his experience of a Nickel raid over Le Mans on the 24th July 1944.

> 'The preliminaries involved much preparation – flight tests, flight plan preparation, the issue of live ammunition and personal emergency kit, then finally a visit from the CO at dispersal before take-off.'

Having completed his initial training in Oxfords, Jack Lunn came to Wing in July 1943 for pilot training in Wellingtons. He recalls his first Operational flight which happened to be a Nickel raid and a rather perilous one at that.

> 'The training was very interesting until one day the games stopped and the real thing was facing us. My first 'op' was from Wing in Wellington BK 490. On returning from a 'Cooks Tour' I was told to go straight for briefing for ops that night. I was a little taken aback thinking that if I was shot down I had not let my mother know what I was up to. However, given a briefing, an orange and a flask of coffee we eventually set off for our distribution area with a load of leaflets for France. Soon after take-off my navigator informed me that he was lost because his Gee-box had packed up. On we went and I flogged the aircraft up to 16000 feet and wondered why it would not go higher, only to find later that this height was its ceiling. I remember looking back at the engines and being frightened to death seeing them red hot and thinking they were on fire. We flew dead reckoning and a coastline appeared which we assumed to be France. After seeing three fighters flying some distance below and on a parallel course to ours, we went into cloud for the rest of the trip. As time was running out for our return we switched on the 11159 and found ourselves smack bang in the London balloon barrage at 5000 feet. Extra revs lifted us to 7000 feet and back to Wing. We were greeted by our C.O. who informed us we were twenty minutes early returning. The navigator was in the bad books and nearly got scrubbed.'

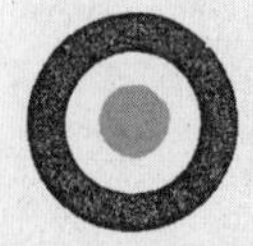

LE COURRIER DE L'AIR

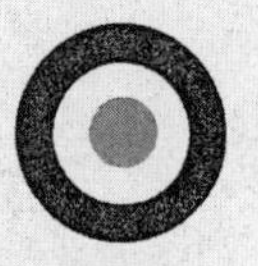

APPORTE PAR LA R.A.F. *LONDRES, LE 22 JUILLET 1943*

L'occupation de la Sicile se poursuit

Le nombre d'Italiens faits prisonniers en Sicile augmente rapidement. En voici quelques uns en route pour l'Afrique du Nord.

LA MOITIÉ ENVIRON DE LA SICILE EST DÉJÀ OCCUPÉE PAR LES ALLIÉS.

Onze jours après les premiers débarquements, ils contrôlent tout le réseau routier et les voies ferrées du sud. Par un mouvement convergent, ils ont avancé sur Enna au centre de l'île, et capturé ce centre nerveux du bastion.

Plus de 40.000 prisonniers sont tombés aux mains des troupes alliées, et leur nombre augmente d'heure en heure.

Dans le secteur de Catane, la VIIIe Armée britannique commandée par le général Montgomery combat contre des troupes allemandes, qui comprennent entre autres, la XVe Division de *panzers* reconstituée. Les Britanniques ont établi une tête de pont et leurs éléments avancés se trouvent, à l'heure actuelle, à quatre kilomètres environ du centre de Catane.

La résistance opiniâtre offerte par les Allemands dans ce secteur semble indiquer qu'ils livrent une bataille destinée à retarder le plus longtemps possible l'avance des Alliés pendant qu'ils achèvent leur dispositif défensif dans la région nord-est de la Sicile, dispositif basé sur Messine et sur la ligne de montagnes de la région.

Un fait frappant est la satisfaction évidente manifestée par les prisonniers italiens d'en avoir fini avec le régime fasciste. Quand ils sont interrogés par les services de renseignement alliés, les Siciliens et même les Italiens du sud font preuve de sentiments anti-fascistes sans équivoque.

Un incident typique de la lassitude des troupes italiennes en Sicile s'est produit au cours de l'avance des troupes américaines et canadiennes sur Enna.

Une compagnie d'Italiens, stationnée sur la route d'Enna, décida de se rendre aux Américains de la VIIe Armée qui s'approchaient d'eux. Un officier allemand protesta. Il fut abattu d'une balle italienne. Les Italiens jetèrent leurs armes et avancèrent vers les Américains, les bras en l'air.

Les sentiments des civils siciliens sont les mêmes que ceux des soldats. Partout la population accueille les Alliés en libérateurs. Lorsqu'un officier britannique lut en public la première proclamation du général Alexander, gouverneur militaire de la Sicile

(Suite à la page 3)

L'initiative est aux Russes

Sur l'ensemble du front en Russie on constate une animation plus marquée.

C'est cependant dans le secteur d'Orel que le combat est le plus dur en ce moment.

Les communiqués du Haut-Commandement russe soulignent que malgré de violentes contre-attaques ennemies, l'Armée rouge avance progressivement, infligeant aux Allemands des pertes sévères en hommes et en matériel.

Il se précise que les Russes attaquent simultanément au nord, au centre et au sud. Des avances ont été realisées dans chacune de ces attaques. Les Russes ont réoccupé quelque 160 villages y compris Malo-Arkhangelskoye et Mtsensk. Cette dernière est située sur la ligne Moscou-Orel.

Les Russes annonçaient le 20 juillet qu'ils avaient capturé trois autres points importants sur la voie ferrée aux alentours d'Orel: Voroshilovo à l'est, Godorische au sud et Ilinskoye au nord. Berlin ne cache pas que le Haut-Commandement allemand n'ignore pas la gravité de la situation.

Au cours des jours qui vont suivre, des développements significatifs pourraient se produire dans le secteur d'Orel.

Dans le Donbas, au sud de Izyoum et au sud-ouest de Voroshilovgrad, il se livre des combats locaux. Dans cette région, les troupes russes ont forcé le passage du Haut Donetz et du Mius, améliorant leurs positions.

L'artillerie lourde russe se montre active dans la région de Krymskaya et de Novorossisk ; au nord-est de cette dernière, les Allemands, comme le signale un communiqué russe, ont lancé plusieurs contre-attaques violentes.

Le Haut-Commandement russe ne mentionne pas le Kouban dans ses compte-rendus. Les Allemands, par contre, font grand état dans leur propagande intérieure des difficultés qu'ils éprouvent à maintenir le ravitaillement de leurs troupes qui occupent la tête de pont du Kouban, du fait que tous les transports venant de la Crimée doivent passer par Kertch.

On sait que la flotte russe domine le détroit, et que les unités navales dont disposent les Allemands ne sont pas de taille à lutter contre elle.

Il semblerait donc que la propagande allemande est en train de préparer la population du Reich aux déboires qui pourraient se produire à l'extrême sud du front.

Le groupe "Normandie" à Orel

Le Groupe "Normandie" qui s'est déjà distingué sur le front russe, participe à l'offensive des Russes contre Orel.

Depuis le 13 juillet, les aviateurs français ont abattu quatre *Messerschmitt* et trois *Focke Wulf*. Le commandant Tulasne, l'as français, s'est adjugé un des appareils.

Plusieurs pilotes du groupe ont déjà à leur actif de nombreux appareils ennemis abattus en France et en Libye.

Nouveaux ministres polonais

Comme il fallait s'y attendre, la mort du général Sikorski des suites d'un accident d'avion a produit un certain flottement au sein du cabinet polonais.

Cette situation a été résolue sur la base d'un accord entre le Président de la République polonaise, M. Raczkiewicz et le Premier Ministre par interim, M. Stanislav Mikolajczyk. Ce dernier a accepté de former un nouveau gouvernement et a eu des conversations avec les représentants des quatre partis politiques polonais en vue de procéder à sa formation.

Le général Kazimierz Sosnkowsky devient Commandant-en-Chef. Les fonctions du Commandant-en-Chef seront strictement militaires.

Bombardement d'objectifs militaires à Rome

En plein jour, le 19 juillet, des formations de bombardiers alliés, au nombre de cinq cents environ, ont attaqué les objectifs militaires suivants à Rome :

Les gares régulatrices de San Lorenzo et de Littorio et l'aéroport de Ciampino.

Les photographies aériennes prises au cours de l'opération démontrent le haut degré de précision réalisé.

La gare de San Lorenzo a été la plus durement atteinte et, pour le moment, le trafic y est entièrement suspendu.

La gare de Littorio a reçu près de cinquante coups directs, et la moitié de sa superficie est bloquée.

Les dégâts à l'aéroport de Ciampino sont lourds. Plusieurs hangars ont été atteints et incendiés et nombre d'avions au sol ont été détruits.

Ainsi se poursuivent méthodiquement les attaques alliées contre le système de transport de l'ennemi.

La bonne aventure

"Les inepties mystiques qui consistent à jongler avec des chiffres pour découvrir les évolutions futures de la guerre font beaucoup pour convaincre les lanceurs de bobards, qui commencent par le Grand Frédéric et Napoléon, pour finir avec la date précise de la fin de la guerre actuelle.

". . . Pour ceux-là, l'histoire ne réside pas dans les peuples, les continents ou les tendances irrésistibles, mais bien dans le marc de café."

(Goebbels dans *Das Reich*.)

F.108

An example of the propaganda leaflets dropped by crews from 26 OTU in Nickel Raids.

Le général Giraud à Londres: *discours radiodiffusé*

PENDANT son séjour à Londres, au cours duquel il a eu des conversations importantes avec M. Churchill, M. Eden et les Chefs d'Etat-Major, le général Giraud a radiodiffusé dans les services d'outremer de la B.B.C.

Voici le texte de son allocution :

"Je me trouvais, il y a quelques jours, dans cette Amérique bourdonnante du bruit des usines de guerre et qui, à une cadence toujours croissante, produit des avions, des tanks, des navires et des régiments.

"Aujourd'hui, c'est de Londres que je vous parle, de ce micro par lequel une équipe de patriotes français, infatigablement, n'a cessé de vous crier les raisons de croire. De Londres où le général de Gaulle rallia l'héroïque avant-garde de l'Armée de la Libération. De Londres qui porte les cicatrices glorieuses des bombardements et qui fut, aux jours les plus sombres, la forteresse de la résistance et de l'espérance.

"C'est ici qu'on mesure le mieux les progrès immenses effectués sur la route de la victoire depuis fin 1940. En défiant l'Allemagne à l'apogée de sa puissance, le pays de Winston Churchill a permis à toutes les forces de la liberté — la Russie, les Etats-Unis, la France d'outremer — de s'armer, de s'unir, de se regrouper. Depuis l'automne dernier, l'initiative est passée de notre côté ; elle y est restée avec l'offensive, avec le succès. Elle y restera.

"Après Stalingrad, Tunis ; après Tunis, la Sicile.

"Les Alliés viennent de réussir là ce que les Allemands n'avaient jamais pu faire malgré leurs vantardises ; faire traverser la mer à plusieurs armées d'un seul coup, débarquer de vive force, établir une tête de pont qui chaque jour se fait plus profonde. Bientôt ce sera le tour de l'Armée française de rentrer en ligne, et cette fois, avec le matériel ultra-moderne dont le Président Roosevelt a bien voulu me promettre d'accélérer la livraison.

En sens inverse

"Vous avez tous encore en tête le souvenir atroce de l'avalanche des *panzers* qui semaient la dévastation sur nos routes. Eh bien ! vous l'entendrez encore ce vacarme, mais en sens inverse quand la ferraille allemande fuira, pourchassée par des chars d'assaut portant les couleurs françaises.

"Après la marée de l'invasion et de l'épouvante, ce sera la vague de la délivrance, du triomphe, qui submergera notre sol. Ceci n'est pas du bourrage de crânes. Ce moment approche avec la certitude précise d'une mécanique d'horloge, ce jour que vous attendez, que j'attends comme vous depuis si longtemps.

Un idéal sacré

"Parmi les soldats que nous sommes, quel est celui qui n'a pas des siens à arracher à la famine, à l'inquiétude mortelle, aux griffes de la *Gestapo* ou des geôliers des *Stalag* et des usines d'Outre-Rhin ?

"Quel est celui qui ne pense pas sans frémir de colère au martyre de la Patrie ? Jamais armée ne sera partie à la bataille animée d'un idéal plus sacré et d'une résolution aussi farouche, car il ne s'agit pas pour nous de conquérir ni même de défendre ; il s'agit de secourir et de délivrer.

A bientôt

"De ce rivage d'Alger que je vais rejoindre, les regards de ces soldats se tendent ardemment vers l'horizon bleu au delà duquel ils devinent, ils entendent la France. La France où se trouvent leurs petits enfants aux joues amaigries, leurs épouses ou leurs vieilles mamans qui font la queue devant des boutiques presque vides, et leurs frères décimés par l'envoi aux travaux forcés.

"La France de la misère, mais aussi la France de la résistance ; la France des camps de concentration et des prisons où l'on fusille à l'aube, mais où dans l'ombre se tisse le réseau toujours plus serré des organisations de combattants sans uniforme.

"C'est pour ce peuple de frères, c'est pour vous, innombrables héros inconnus dont la pensée nous sert de stimulant et d'exemple, que je vais reprendre, là-bas, ma tâche, sans arrêt, sans défaillance.

"L'attente a été, pour moi aussi, longue et sombre, mais maintenant, il me semble apercevoir déjà les clochers de nos villes et de nos villages. . . .

"A bientôt la Lorraine, l'Alsace, la Victoire ! A bientôt la Liberté !

"A bientôt . . . la France ! "

LE NOUVEAU CAMION AMPHIBIE

Les Alliés disposent en quantité illimitée de matériel d'invasion de tout genre. Ci-dessous, un nouveau modèle de camion six roues amphibie de trois tonnes. Debout, le général Montgomery, commandant la VIIe Armée en Sicile.

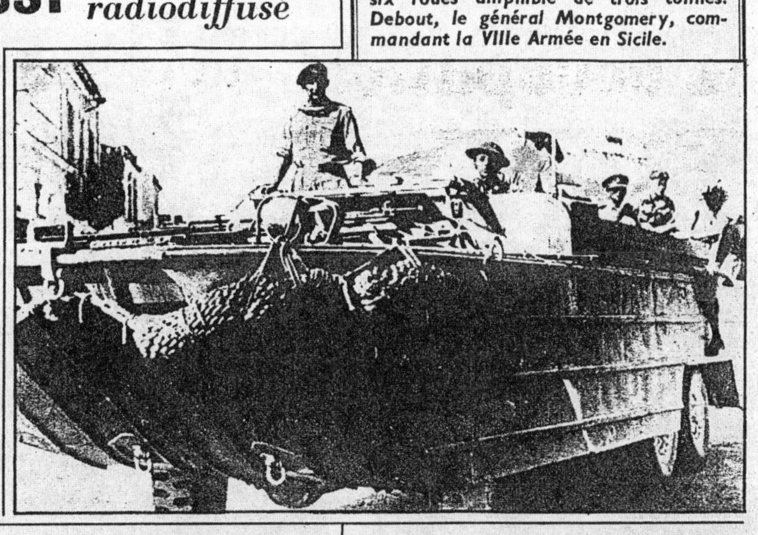

CHANTAGE

Voici une preuve concluante de l'escroquerie à laquelle se livre l'Allemagne, avec la connivence de Laval, sous le prétexte de donner aux prisonniers français en Allemagne le statut d'ouvriers civils.

"Il n'est pas besoin de souligner les avantages que présente cette mesure pour les prisonniers, mesure que le Fuehrer n'a pu consentir au Président Laval que grâce à la sage politique de ce dernier. . . ."

(*L'Oeuvre*, 1er *juin*, 1943)

"Le premier contingent de prisonniers de guerre sont devenus des ouvriers civils dans des entreprises en province. Ce transfert vise à augmenter le rendement des anciens prisonniers de guerre et ainsi d'accroître le potentiel de travail de l'Europe."

(*Königsberge Allgemeine Zeitung*, 28 *juin* 1943.)

Les bombardements aériens

LES bombardiers américains et britanniques qui attaquèrent des bases d'avions allemandes en France le 14 juillet, rencontrèrent une forte opposition de la part des chasseurs ennemis.

Les *Forteresses Volantes* en abattirent quarante-cinq au cours de violents combats au-dessus de Villacoublay et du Bourget.

L'aérodrome et les ateliers d'assemblage et de réparation de Villacoublay sont d'une importance vitale pour la *Luftwaffe*.

Le Bourget est non seulement une base ennemie mais un centre de réserve pour les formations de chasseurs affectées au front de l'ouest.

Ces raids faisaient suite à une autre lourde attaque effectuée par les bombardiers de la *Royal Air Force* contre Aix-la-Chapelle dans la nuit du 13 juillet. Aix-la-Chapelle, important centre ferroviaire de l'Allemagne occidentale, reçut une grande quantité de bombes de quatre tonnes et de bombes incendiaires.

Pour la sixième fois, Munich fut bombardée dans la nuit du 15 juillet. Au cours du raid contre Munich du 9 mars, la Maison Brune, le Quartier-Général nazi, fut endommagée et le bureau personnel d'Hitler détruit par le feu.

D'autre part, des *Lancasters* opérant de Grande-Bretagne, bombardèrent au cours de deux nuits en succession — du 15 et du 16 — des stations de transformateurs en Italie. Leurs principaux objectifs furent Brugherio et Cislago, près de Milan. D'autres objectifs furent atteints près de Bologne. Le bombardement de ces stations électriques, qui commandent le système des chemins de fer électriques italiens, a pour but de disloquer le trafic ferroviaire militaire germano-italien.

Résultats acquis

Le ministère de l'Air britannique vient de révéler l'étendue des dégâts faits à Cologne au cours de trois attaques concentrées par la R.A.F. dans les nuits des 28 juin, 3 et 8 juillet.

Deux usines de l'entreprise Humboldt, fabriquant des Diesels pour sous-marins, ont été sévèrement atteintes.

Douze bâtiments de l'usine de Dentz ont été totalement détruits ou très gravement endommagés.

Les dernières vues prises une semaine après l'attaque montrent que des incendies brûlaient encore dans le dépôt de l'I. G. Farbenindustrie à Leverkusen.

Sept gros bâtiments ont été détruits dans les ateliers de chemin de fer de Nippes.

Salut à la presse clandestine

Le syndicat national des journalistes français s'est regroupé en Afrique française.

Il a constitué à Alger une section des journalistes repliés en collaboration avec les sections d'Afrique du Nord, de l'A.O.F., de l'A.E.F. et de Madagascar.

Le syndicat a adressé ce message à la presse clandestine :

"Le syndicat national des journalistes dirige sa pensée vers tous les membres de la profession qui, en France et dans l'Europe asservie, continuent à combattre pour la cause de la liberté et de la justice, ou sont déjà morts au service de cet idéal. Il salue avec reconnaissance les camarades qui, au mépris de leurs intérêts personnels et même presque toujours de leur sécurité, ont renoncé à l'exercice publique de leur métier pour se consacrer à cette admirable presse clandestine qui entretient et exalte l'esprit de la résistance."

"Italiens, à vous de décider"

NOUS reproduisons ci-dessous le texte de l'appel lancé aux Italiens par M. Churchill et le Président Roosevelt, et radiodiffusé par Alger le 16 juillet :

A l'heure qu'il est, les forces conjuguées des Etats-Unis, de la Grande-Bretagne et du Canada, commandées par le général Eisenhower et son adjoint, le général Alexander, livrent bataille et opèrent une progression profonde sur le territoire de votre pays.

Telle est la conséquence directe de la manière honteuse dont Mussolini et son régime fasciste vous ont gouvernés. Mussolini vous a entraînés dans ce conflit comme satellite d'un assassin des peuples et des libertés.

Mussolini vous a plongés dans une guerre qu'il croyait déjà gagnée par Hitler, sans tenir compte de la grande vulnérabilité de l'Italie en face des attaques aériennes et terrestres ; vos chefs fascistes ont envoyé vos fils, vos navires, vos forces aériennes sur des théâtres d'opération lointains, ceci en vue d'aider l'Allemagne dans sa tentative de conquête de l'Angleterre, de la Russie et du monde.

Cette collaboration aux projets de l'Allemagne nazie était indigne des anciennes traditions de liberté et de culture de l'Italie, auxquels les peuples d'Amérique et de Grande-Bretagne doivent tant.

Ce n'est pas dans l'intérêt de l'Italie que vos soldats se sont battus, mais bien dans celui de l'Allemagne nazie. Ils ont combattu avec courage, mais ils ont été trahis, abandonnés par les Allemands sur le front de Russie et sur tous les champs de bataille, d'El Alamein au Cap Bon.

Aujourd'hui, sur tous les fronts, l'Allemagne voit ses espoirs de conquête mondiale anéantis.

Le ciel italien est à la merci des immenses formations américaines et anglaises. Le littoral italien est menacé par la plus puissante concentration de navires anglais et alliés jamais réalisée dans la Méditerranée.

Le seul espoir

Les forces qui sont entrées en action contre les vôtres sont déterminées à détruire la puissance nazie, utilisée sans scrupules aux fins d'asservir et d'anéantir quiconque refuse de reconnaître les Allemands comme la race suprême.

Le seul espoir de l'Italie de survivre réside dans une capitulation honorable envers la puissance militaire écrasante des Nations Unies. Si vous persistez à tolérer le régime fasciste, qui sert les buts diaboliques du Nazisme, soyez prêts à subir les conséquences de votre décision.

Nous ne tirons nulle satisfaction du fait que nous envahissons le sol italien et que nous apportons au peuple d'Italie le fléau de la guerre et les dévastations qu'il cause, mais nous sommes résolus à abattre les chefs sans conscience, ainsi que leurs doctrines, qui ont placé l'Italie dans la situation où elle se trouve.

Chaque minute de résistance aux forces conjuguées des Nations Unies, chaque goutte de sang ainsi sacrifiée ne peuvent avoir qu'un seul résultat : accorder un peu plus longtemps seulement aux meneurs nazis et fascistes l'illusion qu'ils échapperont aux conséquences inévitables de leurs propres crimes.

Tous vos intérêts, toutes vos traditions ont été trahis par l'Allemagne nazie, et par les mensonges et la corruption de vos propres chefs.

L'Italie ne peut nourrir l'espoir d'occuper un rang respectable dans la famille des nations européennes qu'à la condition de désavouer les nazis et les chefs fascistes.

Italiens, l'heure a sonné pour vous de prendre en considération votre propre dignité, vos intérêts, ainsi que votre désir de vous restaurer l'honneur national, la sécurité et la paix.

C'est à vous de décider, et décider sur l'heure, si les Italiens périront pour Mussolini et Hitler ou s'ils vivront pour l'Italie, pour la civilisation.

L'ORACLE A PARLE

La Stampa, du 10 juillet 1943, publiait un article signé de Mussolini, dans lequel il disait notamment : "Il faut faire une distinction entre 'le débarquement' qui est possible, 'la pénétration' et finalement 'l'invasion.' Il est tout à fait clair que si cette tentative échoue — et j'en suis convaincu — que l'ennemi n'aura plus d'autres atouts avec lesquels battre les puissances tripartites. Il est possible que l'ennemi soit à même d'occuper un lambeau de notre patrie, mais où qu'il l'occupe, il restera à jamais dans la position horizontale, non pas verticale."

Une patrouille alliée à Avola passe les cadavres de soldats italiens morts pour l'Allemagne

Preuve par neuf

"Le rêve de Churchill de débarquer en Italie et de faire de la péninsule une base d'opérations contre le Reich s'est évanoui. Maintenant, l'Italie domine la Méditerranée et, avec l'Allemagne, elle est en train de détruire dans cette partie du monde le centre nerveux de l'Empire britannique."

(*Berliner Boersen Zeitung*, 1er juillet, 1942.)

Chemins de fer stratégiques

GOEBBELS continue d'arguer que la "Forteresse d'Europe" est inexpugnable.

Son argument principal est que le Haut-Commandement allemand dispose de lignes de communications *intérieures* tandis que les Alliés ont le désavantage de combattre sur des lignes *extérieures*.

Un autre son de cloche est donné par le général Hasse dans un article qui a paru dans la *Berliner Boerzen Zeitung* du 29 juin.

Hasse, tout en concédant que des débarquements alliés pourraient réussir dans la période initiale, affirme que l'intervention rapide de réserves mobiles renverserait presque aussitôt la situation en faveur de l'Allemagne.

La doctrine militaire a toujours considéré la concentration de l'effort comme la condition *sine qua non* du succès. Il serait donc normal que l'Etat-Major allemand, malgré les circonstances défavorables, fasse de gros efforts pour conserver dans sa stratégie le maximum de concentration.

Mais l'existence en Allemagne ou en Europe centrale d'une puissante masse de manœuvre peut être mise en doute à la lumière des faits suivants.

Un examen détaillé de l'ordre de bataille allemand *à l'heure actuelle* révèle que le gros des troupes stationnées en Allemagne se compose d'unités administratives ou d'instruction. Plus de 95% des forces de campagne allemandes sont déjà disposés sur les trois grands fronts défensifs : la Russie, l'Europe occidentale, la Méditerranée, d'où il sera extrêmement difficile de les retirer.

Pourquoi l'Allemagne, qui théoriquement tirerait grand profit d'une réserve centrale, a-t-elle dû, en fait, mépriser cet avantage ?

La raison en est apparemment que le Haut-Commandement allemand n'a qu'une confiance limitée dans la capacité du réseau ferré européen à donner à cette réserve la mobilité nécessaire.

Il cherche donc à réduire, dans la mesure du possible, l'interdépendance de sa stratégie et du réseau ferré.

En fait, les dispositions prises par l'ennemi ne diminuent en rien l'importance majeure de ses transports ferroviaires car :

1. le Reich demeure l'arsenal et la base principale de toutes les armées allemandes,
2. Les territoires où sont disposés les divers groupes d'armées sont très vastes, et le mouvement des troupes continuera à s'y faire en majeure partie par chemin de fer, et,
3. L'Allemagne sera contrainte, tôt ou tard, à mesure que le plan allié sera mis à exécution, d'en revenir au transfert de divisions d'un théâtre européen à l'autre, *à un moment décisif*.

Le Haut-Commandement allemand n'ignore certes pas ce jugement de Ludendorff : "Il arrive un moment dans toutes les guerres où les locomotives deviennent plus importantes que les canons".

Ce moment approche, et l'action des patriotes des pays occupés épaule largement la campagne offensive menée à fond par la R.A.F., l'aviation américaine et les forces aériennes soviétiques, non seulement contre les locomotives et le matériel roulant, mais aussi contre les centres de production et de réparation de matériel ferroviaire.

Joie des Siciliens

(SUITE DE LA PAGE I)

occupée (voir plus loin), la foule applaudit et montra ouvertement sa joie.

Dans toute la partie de l'île occupée par les Alliés, l'ordre règne parmi la population. Les emblèmes du régime fasciste et les portraits de Mussolini sont retirés et détruits.

Dans sa première proclamation le général Alexander, gouverneur militaire de la Sicile, a ordonné la dissolution du parti fasciste et a annulé les lois racistes.

La proclamation ordonne également l'application des mesures suivantes :—

1. Les pouvoirs de gouvernement et de juridiction sont remis au général commandant et gouverneur général.

2. L'exercice des pouvoirs de la Couronne d'Italie est suspendu durant l'occupation militaire.

3. Les droits personnels et les droits de propriété seront pleinement respectés.

Le général Alexander promet à la population de la Sicile que tant qu'elle se montrera paisible et se soumettra aux ordres, nul n'interviendra dans son existence au-delà de ce qu'exigent les nécessités militaires. Les Siciliens pourront "vaquer à leurs occupations sans crainte".

Complainte de la Wehrmacht

C'est Hitler qui nous mène,
C'est Goebbels qui parle pour nous,
C'est Goering qui mange pour nous,
C'est Ley qui boit pour nous,
Mais personne ne meurt pour nous.

Eclaircissement

"Il a été rabâché au peuple britannique que l'industrie de guerre de la Grande-Bretagne peut fabriquer des chars comme des petits pains. Qu'est-ce que les Britanniques vont faire de tout ce matériel de guerre ? "

(*Radio-Rome*, 1er juillet, 1942.)

LE COURRIER DE L'AIR

"Pacte d'acier"

En Sicile, les Italiens ont pu, depuis le 10 juillet, mesurer toute l'envergure de la tâche qui les confronte.

Nous disons bien ... les Italiens, car Stillfried, le commentateur de Trans-ocean *vient de le leur rappeler avec une candeur brutale dans sa revue hebdomadaire : "En ce qui concerne l'Italie," écrit-il, "la guerre a été jusqu'ici pour elle une guerre coloniale. Maintenant les Italiens doivent défendre leur pays."*

Cette assertion venant s'ajouter aux souvenirs amers de El Alamein et de Tunisie, ne plaira pas aux Italiens qui ont servi de chair à canon en Russie.

Elle plaira encore moins aux soldats italiens, qui, immobilisés en Yougoslavie et en Grèce, mènent une existence rendue périlleuse par l'action vengeresse des patriotes.

Quant aux populations italiennes — que Scorza menacent aujourd'hui de ses foudres si elles ne résistent pas jusqu'au bout — elles doivent arriver à la conclusion que, sans Mussolini et sa ribambelle de pantins corrompus, elles n'auraient pas besoin de défendre leur pays.

Un peu tard, l'Italie se rend compte que son fameux "pacte d'acier" avec l'Allemagne a été mal trempé, et que toutes les pailles se trouvent, comme par hasard, dans l'exemplaire dont Mussolini a doté ses dupes.

* * *

Mais il n'est pas trop tard pour remédier à cet état de choses.

M. Churchill et le Président Roosevelt ont adressé à la nation italienne une mise en demeure.

En admettant même que les Allemands viennent à l'aide du fascisme italien chancelant, ils sont trop engagés en Russie, et menacés ailleurs pour lui envoyer une aide efficace.

L'appel des Alliés stipule clairement qu'une Italie, purgée du fascisme, pourra retrouver une place respectable dans l'Europe libérée.

C'est aux Italiens de choisir :

Ou bien ils capitulent honorablement, en s'en remettant à l'honneur et à la justice des vainqueurs.

Ou bien ils continuent une lutte sans espoir, et dans ce cas ils verseront leur sang au seul profit d'une Allemagne qui les méprise et les traite en valets.

"J'ai vu débarquer les Alliés"

Par un officier de la Royal Navy

La flotte d'invasion, composée de plus de deux mille navires de toutes sortes et de toutes tailles, se rassembla dans divers ports de l'Afrique du Nord et de la Grande-Bretagne.

Les troupes furent dirigées vers les camps préparés à l'avance, et, ayant achevé leur instruction et leur entraînement, elles attendaient le jour "J" en se distrayant comme elles le pouvaient, surtout en se baignant dans le bleu azur de la Méditerranée.

Le 10 juillet l'ordre fut donné d'appareiller. Nous faisions route vers le point de ralliement. La flotte dont nous faisions partie semblait être, à elle seule, suffisante pour effectuer l'invasion. Et pourtant, nous savions pertinamment que nous n'étions qu'une infime fraction du tout.

A cette époque de l'année, le temps en Méditerranée est généralement beau et calme. Mais subitement le vent se mit à souffler en demi-tempête du nord-ouest. Il fallait donc s'attendre à ce que les plages siciliennes fussent balayées par les brisants ; nos chalands allaient être confrontés par une tâche presque impossible à accomplir.

Nous espérions qu'avec le coucher du soleil le vent tomberait ; bien au contraire, les bourrasques se succédaient de plus en plus fortes.

Puis survint le miracle. Une heure et demi à peine avant l'heure "H," le vent s'abattait et les moutons disparaissaient. La houle elle-même se calmait avec une rapidité telle que je n'avais jamais vue.

Aucun signe d'avions ennemis dans un ciel étoilé et éclairé d'une demi-lune. Comme nous arrivions dans les parages de la côte, nos bombardiers, en route pour Syracuse, ronronnaient au-dessus de nous. Des projecteurs s'allumèrent ; des balles traceuses et des obus de D.C.A. sillonnaient l'obscurité.

Peu après, les éclairs des explosions de nos bombes illuminaient la nuit, suivis du rougeoiment des incendies qu'elles avaient allumés. Puis, de gros avions de transport, chargés de parachutistes, passèrent suivis d'autres appareils remorquant les planeurs remplis de troupes aéroportées.

Au-dessus de la Sicile, des avions jetaient des fusées éclairantes qui ressemblaient à de gigantesques lampions. Par hasard, le centre d'une ligne de fusées descendait plus vite que les ailes, le tout formant un "V" géant rutilant de lumière.

Tous feux éteints, chaque bâtiment à son poste exact, la flotte la plus puissante de l'histoire s'approchait de la Sicile. Au coucher de la lune, la sirène du bateau-amiral retentit.

Ça y était ! L'heure "H" avait sonné.

Suspendus à leurs bossoirs, les chalands bondés d'hommes étaient prêts à prendre la mer. Après quelques à coups occasionnés par la houle, tous étaient à flot et mettaient le cap sur la plage.

Dans tout débarquement, le temps semble interminable à ceux qui restent à bord pendant que les embarcations accomplissent le trajet entre le navire et la grève. Ceux à bord des chalands n'ont rien d'autre à faire que de rester assis dans l'attente que les batteries côtières ouvrent le feu.

Enfin, la tension se dispersa. Les premiers chalands touchèrent le fond et les hommes se jetèrent par-dessus bord et prirent pied avec l'eau aux aisselles. L'offensive était déclenchée.

L'ennemi, jeté dans la confusion par la quantité de bateaux qui participaient à l'opération, tirait éperdument dans toutes les directions. Mais du moment où elles ouvrirent le feu, les casemates furent repérées et pilonnées par les canons des contre-torpilleurs de couverture.

Les hommes avaient reçu ordre de ménager leurs munitions ; aussi, se lancèrent-ils à l'assaut à la baïonnette. Au fur et à mesure de la réduction des îlots de résistance la liaison annonçait la capture des premiers objectifs.

Au point du jour, des volutes de fumée tourbillonnaient au-dessus de la côte. Quand le soleil se leva, nous vîmes un spectacle qui nous fit écarquiller les yeux. A perte de vue s'alignaient des navires, d'autres navires et toujours des navires. Il y avait des gros transports qui déchargeaient des troupes, des contre-torpilleurs qui canonnaient l'ennemi, des dragueurs de mines qui nettoyaient les chenaux pour les chalands. Il y en avait de toutes sortes — des porte-chars, des porte-canons, des transbordeurs de camions et de voitures tous terrains, des chalands d'approvisionnement ...

Dès qu'ils s'approchaient des plages, des officiers-contrôleurs les guidaient à leur emplacement ; les rampes étaient abaissées et troupes et véhicules débarquaient et s'engageaient dans les routes qui mènent à l'intérieur de la Sicile.

Ce fut un chef-d'œuvre d'entraînement et d'organisation.

Autour de cette agglomération maritime, des contre-torpilleurs patrouillaient, guettant les sous-marins ennemis, tandis que les *Spitfires* et autres chasseurs veillaient, prêts à foncer sur les bombardiers ennemis.

De l'intérieur venait le grondement des bombes jetées par nos avions sur les positions ennemies.

Les sapeurs du génie déblayaient les champs de mines ennemis, marquant d'un cordon blanc le chemin qu'ils avaient frayé aux troupes impatientes de se mesurer avec les défenseurs.

Et en mer, à perte de vue, flottaient des drapeaux britanniques et américains.

Opinion was divided as to the efficacy of these propaganda leaflets. One school of thought was that they provided Europe with a year's supply of toilet paper in one night! However it was considered by others that this type of sortie was a valuable introduction to ops over Europe. As well as completing the mission successfully it was also expected that a picture be taken to show where the aircraft dropped the leaflets.

Another form of operation was the Diversionary Raid or Feint where aircraft flew along the French coast to keep the enemy radar busy in a certain area whilst the main force flew inland to bomb a target.

Keith McLean remembers an amusing incident relating to this,

> 'On one occasion we were needed for a Diversionary Raid where we were to drop 'Window' (i.e.Metallised strips) to misinform the enemy radar and allow the main force through. Normally there were two diversionary streams so that any German fighters would be split in order to follow them and in so doing would not only reduce the number of fighters available to attack the main force but would also use up the fighters' fuel. It was to be our first flight over enemy territory. It was wet and we taxied around the perimeter track but the Captain decided to take a short cut over the grass and we became bogged down. We never did take off and we were picked up in a truck driven by a WAAF.'

It so happened that the aircraft that did take off on the exercise were meant to fly at maximum height but dense cloud and icing forced them all to return.

Denis Down, a Navigator who was at Wing during August – November 1944 also remembers taking part in a 'Feint' exercise.

> 'It was a special exercise on 14th October executed as part of the final training, being mainly a series of long Cross-country flights. There was a big Bomber Command attack on Duisburg that night so we were required to divert the German defences from that attack by our approach to their Northern Coast.'

His crewmates on that exercise were Lex Howell RAAF – Captain, Ken Poole – Bomb Aimer, Peter Weston – Wireless Operator, Bill Hughes – Mid Upper Gunner and Bernie Kaye – Rear Gunner.

CHAPTER 11
Time Marches on – 1943

In January 1943 Group Captain J. Bradbury from RAF Marston Moor took over command of 26 OTU from Group Captain Park who had moved on to 92 Group HQ at Winslow Hall. Bradbury made an immediate impression by addressing all officers, Warrant Officers, NCOs and other ranks at both Wing and Little Horwood during his first week in command.

By February the Unit received its first intake of Wellington III bombers. These gradually replaced the older 1Cs, some of which were passed on to other OTUs although many were to remain in service at Wing throughout the year. Ten Mk IIIs were initially received to supplement the fifty-two 1Cs, whilst in March a further sixteen arrived with the influx of new arrivals continuing into May.

Early in the month Wing became a short-term base for two squadrons of Mustang Mk1s on tactical reconnaissance and ground attack duty. And short-term it really was, as 268 and 613 squadrons remained only from 1st to the 6th of the month during a series of rapid deployments.

March also saw a new feature in the form of a regular News sheet wittily entitled Wingspan. This was displayed on prominent noticeboards and in the messes and NAAFIs, and was no doubt welcomed as a means of informing all personnel of news and events at the Unit.

Training, of course, continued at maximum level and as well as the flying elements already mentioned there were numerous other types such as Anti-Gas Warfare Training and Gas Chamber Tests. George Bignell remembers well an exercise involving the use of mustard gas,

> 'The gas was sprayed into a Wellington and we all had to wear gas masks and protective clothing. It was a hot and sticky day and I was stuck in the cockpit to release the brakes when the plane had to be moved.The ground crew had to use a steam jenny to clean up with special liquid. I was in there for two hours!'

On a lighter note, the walls of the main dining room and WAAFs' mess (and probably others) were brightened by the painting of murals which were the handiwork of a certain WAAF, Aircraftwoman Bird. That in the WAAF mess, a flamenco dancer, can still be seen faintly, the building now being used as a workshop. Equally intriguing was the news reported in the ORB that a pie making machine had been installed in the kitchen,

> 'it is hoped with great benefit and economy.'

Continuing on the food theme, the YMCA Canteen was opened on 1st June.

During that same month No.1684 Bomber Defence Training Flight was formed at Little Horwood under the command of Flight Lieutenant F.A.Bernard. Six Tomahawks made up its force initially, with its role being to train aircrews in defensive tactics. On the 17th July, 1684 Flight moved to Wing.

At the end of August Operational Flying was resumed whilst Nickel sorties began over France and continued to the end of the year.(See 26 OTU In Action).

September saw a Colour Hoisting Parade to mark Battle Of Britain Day (15th), whilst a similar event took place at Little Horwood. At Wing the command was for all to attend apart from certain duty officers and aircrew who had been flying after midnight on the previous day. The Parade was made up of six flights as listed below.

No 1 Flight – led by NCO in charge – Sgt Wilson.
No 2 Flight – led by Sgt Harris and WAAFs.
No 3 Flight – led by W/O Taylor with A Flight Maintenance and Servicing Flight.
No 4 Flight – led by W/O Jolly with B and E Flight Maintenance and Servicing Flights.
No 5 Flight – led by W/O Crump with Training Wing from A Flight including all instructors.
No 6 Flight – led by W/O White (as above, B Flight).

A note was also included in the orders of the day stating that Jewish and Roman Catholic personnel could absent themselves from the parade, although the Station Commander was keen that all should attend as it was a non-denominational event.

As the month progressed twelve Wellington Mk X bombers were added to the Unit's equipment alongside forty-one Mark IIIs, as well as two Ansons, four Martinets for gunnery training, two Proctors, two Tutors, the six Tomahawks mentioned earlier, one Tiger Moth, one Oxford, and one Cygnet.

A further parade took place on the 27th November with 12 flights included, in which the Station Chaplain, the Reverend G.S.Froggat, conducted morning prayers after the hoisting of the Colours. The Commanding Officer then inspected four flights before taking the salute at the march past at the end of the parade. The photographs included (page 11) are a unique reminder of this the first of the Station monthly Parades and give a glimpse of not only the large numbers of personnel but also Hangars 1 and 2.

CHAPTER 12
Return to Bombing Operations 1943

In August 1943 the Unit was requested to provide aircraft and crews for a series of small raids on ammunition dumps located in various forests in Northern France. A small number of Pathfinder aircraft marked each target and one of the purposes of the raids was to accustom OTU crews to bombing on to markers before being posted to front line squadrons.

The first of these raids took place on the night of 30th/31st August with 33 Wellington aircraft being supplied by OTUs, whilst Mosquitoes and Halifaxes were provided by the Pathfinder Squadrons. The target was an ammunition dump in the Foret d'Eperlecques, just north of St Omer. Of the aircraft that set out, just two failed to return, with one of these being from 26 OTU. It was one of only four from the Unit to be involved. Despite this the mission was considered to be successful with a large explosion observed. The aircraft and crews from the Unit were as follows:

HE 500 Wellington X

After take-off at 2100 this aircraft was reported missing with no W/T message received and nothing seen of it. In fact the aircraft crashed at Rubrouck, 10km north-west of Cassell, with no survivors.

The crew were:

Sgt K. Knaggs	– Captain
P/O R.P.F. Durne	– Navigator
Sgt L.M. Lewis	– Air Bomber
Sgt P.R. Hogan	– W/Op – Air Gunner
Sgt C. Hayhurst	– Mid-Upper Gunner
Sgt E. Pursell	– Air Gunner

The Navigator is buried at Rubrouck Cemetery, whilst the rest of the crew are buried in the Longuenesse Souvenir Cemetery at St Omer.

HE 479 Wellington X

This aircraft actually took part in all three of the raids in which 26 OTU were involved at this time. A successful mission is recorded in the Operations Record Book, with six 500lb bombs having hit the target area. The crew, who were also to take this aircraft on the next raid were:

Sgt W.Palmer – Captain
Sgt F.A. Easthorpe – Navigator
Sgt H. Beasley – Air Bomber
Sgt F.A. Hayward – W/Op – Air Gunner
Sgt F.H.J. Paul – Mid-Upper Gunner
Sgt L.H. Hood – Air Gunner

BK 275 Wellington III

A successful mission was reported with bombs having been dropped on target and seen to explode. The crew, as with the others involved in these raids, were probably the most experienced at the Unit and would soon be expecting to transfer to Squadrons. This particular crew were to be involved in the next raid also but in a different aircraft.

F/L R.O. Francis – Captain
P/O G.G. Wileman – Navigator
Sgt G. Evans – Air Bomber
Sgt R. Kennedy – W/Op-Air Gunner
Sgt F. Love – Mid-Upper Gunner
Sgt A.E. Hill – Air Gunner

The aircraft, which was not used on subsequent raids, had previously been with both 75 and 115 Squadrons before seeing service at Wing. Here it remained until it was struck off charge on 5th July 1945 having survived a minor accident in October 1943.

X3818 Wellington III

Up at 2125, the last of the four to leave from Wing, this aircraft successfully bombed the target area and returned between 2345 and 2355 as did the three other survivors.

The crew:

Sgt R.E. Plowright – Captain
Sgt N.H.B. Lucas – Navigator
Sgt R.P. Allen – Air Bomber
Sgt H. Hannah – W/Op-Air Gunner
Sgt N.F. Wells – Mid-Upper Gunner
Sgt F. Corr – Air Gunner

The second raid took place on the night of 2nd/3rd September with various OTUs providing 30 Wellington bombers, whilst the Pathfinders supplied six Mosquitoes and five Lancasters. The target on this occasion was an ammunition dump in the Foret de Mormal. 26 OTU provided only three aircraft and crews on this raid.

HE479 Wellington X

The same crew that enjoyed the successful previous mission were to repeat the achievement this time round.

BJ 978 Wellington III

Another successful mission was reported by this crew who had flown in BK 275 on the previous raid. The aircraft which had previously been with 29 OTU remained in service with the Unit until closure in May 1946 and was finally struck off charge in May 1947. This may not have been the case however, had it not been lucky to survive a training accident when involved in a Bullseye exercise on 29th January 1944. When off course over London the aircraft was hit by Anti-Aircraft fire at a time when enemy aircraft were active. There appears to have been no serious injury to the crew members.

BJ 717 Wellington III

Another successful mission was recorded by this crew who were to fly in BK 191 on the next raid which involved 26 OTU.

Sgt J.L. Kennedy – Captain
Sgt J.E. Drag – Navigator
Sgt A.E. Brown – Air Bomber
Sgt A.W. Miller – W/Op-Air Gunner
Sgt H.H. Falls – Mid Upper Gunner
Sgt H.S. Andrews – Air Gunner

A third raid on the Foret de Raismes near Valenciennes did not actually involve the Unit but they were soon in action again on the night of the 8th/9th September 1943. The Bomber Command War Diaries give details of a much larger operation on this night but do not refer to any small scale raid such as the previous ones mentioned. The Operations Record Book does not include the target for this special mission, so it might be assumed that the Unit contributed to this larger raid on long range gun batteries situated near Boulogne. Two hundred and fifty-seven aircraft were involved including 119 Wellingtons along with Stirlings, Mosquitoes, Halifaxes and five B-17 Bombers. This was the first occasion in which the Americans joined night bombing sorties with Bomber Command. The raid, however, proved unsuccessful with inaccurate marking and bombing and it appears that the battery remained undamaged.

The aircraft and crews involved from the Unit were:

HE 479 Wellington X

A new crew climbed aboard for this the aircraft's third bombing mission with the Unit.

P/O T. Moore – Captain
P/O J. Lindley – Navigator

Sgt L. Woodruff – Air Bomber
Sgt A. Cardiff – W/Op-Air Gunner
Sgt B. Town – Air Gunner
Sgt R. Bentley – Mid Upper Gunner

BK 398 **Wellington III**

This aircraft was crewed by those who previously flew in BJ 717 on the previous raid involving 26 OTU. It had been acquired from 16 OTU and was later to see service with both 29 and 86 OTUs before being struck off charge on 12.5.47.

BK 398 **Wellington III**

This aircraft had previously been with 424 Squadron and was to remain with the Unit until closure. The crew for this raid were:

Sgt Sargent – Captain
Sgt C. Westaby – Navigator
Sgt S. Baker-George – Air Bomber
Sgt R. Horwood – W/Op-Air Gunner
Sgt S. Carne – Air Gunner
Sgt R. O'Grady – Mid Upper Gunner

BK 440 **Wellington III**

The crew for this raid were once again flying on their first bombing operation. They were:

Sgt G. Highton – Captain
Sgt F. Webber – Navigator
Sgt M. Clarke – Air Bomber
Sgt A. Atkiss – W/Op-Air Gunner
Sgt R. Shirley – Air Gunner
Sgt K. Horgan – Mid Upper Gunner

The aircraft returned safely from the operation but was to be destroyed in a training accident on 4.12.43. (details in Appendix 2)

This raid proved to be the final bombing operation involving 26 OTU. Other operational flying including Nickel sorties, feints etc did continue from Wing during the year.

CHAPTER 13
Arthur Aaron – A Story of Great Courage

During its short lifetime, over a thousand young men passed through 26 OTU and despite the terrible loss of too many of these in terrible accidents, the vast majority progressed to join squadrons ready for front line action.

Undoubtedly, there are many stories to be told of the action in which these men were involved. There will be stories of great bravery, courage and daring, of narrow escapes, tragedy and disaster – enough probably to fill many a volume.

This is one of those stories and perhaps one of the most remarkable. It involves a pilot by the name of Arthur Aaron and for his extreme courage he was awarded the highest honour – the Victoria Cross.

Arthur Aaron was born in Leeds on 5th March 1922 and became fascinated by flying in his youth. Along with mountains and rock climbing, flying became a passion, especially after experiencing the thrill of a short flight with a travelling aerial circus.

Educated at Roundhay Secondary School, Aaron won an art scholarship in 1939 and entered Leeds College of Architecture as the start of his intended career. His love of flying remained, however, and he joined the Leeds University Squadron of the Air Defence Corps before eventually enlisting in the RAF for pilot training on 15 September 1941.

In December of that year Aaron was sent to the USA and began flying instruction at No. 1 (British) Flying Training School in Terrell, Texas, where he graduated as a sergeant Pilot in June the following year. On his return to England, Aaron underwent further enhanced instruction at No.6 (P) AFU before arriving at 26 OTU towards the end of 1942. From here he moved on to 1657 HCU to acquire experience in handling the giant four engined Short Stirling bomber and on completion of his training he joined 218 'Gold Coast' Squadron, based at Downham Market, on 17th April 1943.

Aaron's first operational sortie involved dropping mines in the Bay Of Biscay and from this very first operation he began to display the characteristics of a capable and strong leader. He demanded even more efficiency from his crew, insisting that each gained some experience of the jobs of the other members, thus leading to improved understanding and co-operation. Aaron felt this would enable any of the crew to cope with any situation they might find themselves in.

On 1 May 1943 Aaron was promoted to Flight Sergeant and during the following three months he and his crew completed twenty sorties over Europe. On one of these their aircraft was damaged by flak yet, undeterred, the objective was bombed and a safe return was made. For his action Aaron was awarded the DFM.

The crew's twenty first sortie was on 12 August 1943 and in the afternoon briefing they were informed that the target was Turin. This was their first trip to Italy and they took off from

Downham Market that evening in Stirling EF452 HA-0. The Navigator was Sergeant Bill Brennan, a Canadian, with his countryman, Flight Sergeant Allan Laren, the Bomb Aimer. Sergeant T. 'Jimmy' Guy was the Wireless Operator, with Sergeant Malcolm Mitchem, the Flight Engineer whilst the two Gunners of the crew were J. Richmond, in the mid-upper gun turret and Sergeant Thomas McCabe in the rear gun turret. All were experienced men who knew their jobs thoroughly and had been well briefed for the mission.

Aaron took the Stirling over the Alps and after remarking on the beauty of the scene, headed for Turin, where, on approaching the city he ordered the bomb doors to be opened, and Larden and Mitchen took up their positions ready for the drop.

Before they could proceed, however, a fellow Stirling was observed slightly below and rather too close on the starboard side and then even more alarmingly opened fire on them from about 250 yards. It was 0120 on Friday 13 August.

Before they could come to terms with events, Brennan had been killed and Aaron had been badly injured with blood pouring from a gaping wound in the face and his right arm dangling limp and useless, held on by only a few tendons. The instrument panel had been smashed and shattered, while the pilot's side of the front windscreen was blown apart and with the inboard engine throttle levers badly bent, the Stirling went into a 250mph dive.

Mitchem, in the right hand pilot's seat, fought to straighten the plunging bomber and was soon assisted by Larden who regained control of the aircraft, levelling at about 4, 000 feet above the Alps. Meanwhile, Mitchem and his crewmates prepared to give Aaron morphine injections and moved him amidships but before they did so, the skipper, who amazingly was still conscious, scribbled a message telling Larden to head for England.

But Larden had little option at that moment, other than to head south over and through the mountains, constantly fighting for control of the crippled bomber. The automatic pilot was inoperable, the rear turret useless and the starboard inner engine was threatening to overheat. There was also the concern that a full bomb load was still on board. Larden managed to take the aircraft in an eastward direction and then turned west in an attempt to reach British occupied territory in Sicily. The possibility of bailing out was considered but it was decided this would be too dangerous and the crew were not prepared to risk further injury to Aaron.

Jimmy Guy continued to transmit to base but the response was virtually inaudible. They were alone in the sky without a position fix or accurate course to fly and having little idea of their precise location.

The flight continued and crossed the Italian coast at Spezia where Larden jettisoned the bomb load over the harbour area. First Mitchem, then Richmond, took turns at piloting whilst parachutes and dinghies were checked for damage and prepared for use.

Having sent out a distress call to Bone airfield in North Africa, the crew were relieved to receive a reply which suggested they endeavour to cross the Mediterranean and land at the airfield. Both Larden and Mitchem had been hit during the original 'attack', the former having two bullets in his right buttock, whilst the latter had been hit in the ankle, his right flying boot cut in two.

At this time Aaron had regained consciousness and Guy and Richmond were able to reassure their skipper that they were on course for Bone airfield and had a map bearing to get them there. For nearly four hours they continued across the Mediterranean with Larden and Mitchem ensuring that no petrol was wasted by alternating engine power and carefully extracting the last drop from each tank in turn.

At last a lighted landing strip came into view and Larden prepared to land. A message from the aerodrome warned of the presence of a crashed Wellington at the end of the runway so Larden decided to make a wheels-up landing alongside the runway.

Astonishingly, Aaron heaved himself forward to take command of the landing and the two gunners helped him into the pilot's seat, whilst Larden eased himself into that of the co-pilot. Aaron had only his left arm to operate the controls and being unable to talk could only communicate by nodding his head and using this method, he indicated to Larden to take the aircraft round again in order to prepare for landing.

On the second approach Aaron was again not satisfied and signalled to Larden to open up and circuit. At this time, Mitchem expressed concern that the fuel supply had virtually gone and that it was imperative they landed this time. The Stirling made its third approach but, at only 500 feet, Aaron indicated to Larden to go round yet again. Larden replied that the fuel position would not allow this, only for Aaron to pull on the throttle seemingly unable to comprehend.

In desperation Larden thumped Aaron on the chest to make him release the controls. Larden then pushed the control column hard forward and held tight as the aircraft skidded in a belly landing, before coming to rest.

Aaron was rushed to the hospital on the base where surgeons operated to remove bullets from the right chest cavity. The remaining crewmen were checked and treated for minor wounds but that afternoon they received the terrible news that their skipper had died from his appalling injuries.

Arthur Aaron was buried with full military honours at Bone cemetery and on 3 November 1943 the London Gazette published the official citation for the award of a posthumous Victoria Cross.

For their part in this courageous action, Allan Larden was awarded a CGM – Conspicuous Gallantry Medal – whilst Mitchem and Guy each received a DFM.

On 25th February 1944 Aaron's parents received their son's award at a Buckingham Palace investiture. The story does not end there though, because, two years later, the Aarons' house was burgled and all of Arthur Aaron's medals stolen. After a police appeal the medals were eventually returned anonymously through the post and in 1953 Aaron's father presented them to Leeds City Museum for permanent display.

In a letter to Aaron's parents, Sir Arthur Harris, Commander-In-Chief of RAF Bomber Command wrote,

> 'In my opinion, never even in the annals of the RAF, has the VC been awarded for skill, determination and courage in the face of the enemy of a higher order than that displayed by your son on his last flight'.

The official citation of the award of the posthumous Victoria Cross attributed the attack on the aircraft to 'an enemy nightfighter.'

CHAPTER 14
WAAFs at Wing

As at all OTUs the contribution of the WAAFs should never be underestimated. They were involved in a wide range of activities from aspects of clerical work to 'fabric bashers' repairing aircraft, from drivers to teleprinter operators, from cooks to wireless operators and numerous other 'trades' between. They were often expected to turn their hand to aspects of work other than the one they might have specific training in, for as the ORB reports in January 1944:

> 'on returning from leave WAAFs will be detailed for one day's duty to the Section in which assistance is most needed.'

Although originally billetted near to the Communal Site, the girls were soon moved to the site nearest to Wing on the Cublington Road, much of which still stands today. The only problem regarding this was the distance from the airfield itself. Denise Cramp (nee Simmons) was Secretary to Wing Commander Gardner in charge of Maintenance Wing and recalls that,

A group of unknown WAAFs at RAF Wing. (J.P.)

'the original WAAF Site was miles away from anything else, situated in cornfields beyond the Communal Site before we were moved to the Cublington Road. This Site was again miles away; it was obviously felt that the women should be well segregated.'

The distance from the main camp and airfield is well remembered also by Joan Greenacre (nee Webdale) an MT Driver who was at the Unit from its early days.

'It was a dispersed aerodrome and as usual the WAAF quarters were away from the main camp, so we were issued with bicycles. It was difficult to get batteries though and if you left them or the pump on the bike they of course disappeared!'

Pat Richards (nee Boyd) who was a wireless operator in Flying Control remembers that it was soon realised that the distance caused problems for some of the girls.

'As we did shift duties they moved us Signal girls closer to the airfield by putting us on the Communal Site.'

Another problem, especially on dark nights and without bicycle lights, was the journey back to the main WAAF Site. Denise Cramp recalls one bizarre incident.

'One night when cycling back to the Site in the pitch black a WAAF friend and I collided with a cow. What followed was a night in Sick Bay and for my pal a broken ankle!'

The Nissen Huts themselves also created the occasional difficulty as Joan Green recalls.

'They could be very cold in winter as they were unlined. On one occasion we could not get the boiler type fire to go because the chimney was sooted up and after a particularly cold night we decided something had to be done. The next evening one of us was up on the chimney and dangled a piece of rope with a brick on the end down it. The soot was soon cleared and fell into the fireplace.'

The girls however were pleased that they were

'treated more or less like the men,'

although an amusing report in the ORB would suggest that there were occasions when this was not so.

On the 13th October 1944 a secret blanket check was undertaken involving 30 Officers and 30 NCOs.

'At 0530, 0540 and 0550 a Tannoy broadcast was put out to inform all personnel except WAAFs and those on duty to stand by their beds for inspection. It was a great success, 90% of the victims being so dazed as to be unable to hinder or frustrate our aims. A small percentage threw a few surplus blankets out of the windows whilst 28 were found hidden in an air-raid shelter. Every building was combed and few, if any, blankets got away. The WAAFs having already had their inventory exhaustively checked were not brought into the scheme and it is understood they snuggled down under adequate supplies of blankets and chortled with glee at the broadcasts.'

Although there was a mess on the WAAF Site Joan recalls that it was not always functioning and it was necessary to cycle to the Airmen's Mess to eat.

'As this was a cycle trip away we often missed breakfast and hoped to catch the NAAFI van as it did its rounds later in the morning.'

Denise adds that the food

> 'wasn't too bad and we were always hungry, but not through a lack of food.'

The WAAF Mess was actually closed for more than a year, only re-opening in December 1944.

Being an MT Driver enabled Joan Greenacre to become familiar with the local area as there were regular runs to Leighton Buzzard, either to the Main Post Office on the postal run or the railway station on the postings run, the latter necessitating the collection or dropping off of personnel. There were also runs to a variety of nearby depots for supplies. Joan has a distinct memory of some important supplies that were obtained on these runs.

> 'On the return journey from the Main Post Office it was commonplace to stop at Faulkners in Linslade for their delicious bread rolls whilst the girls on the coal lorries would be expected to organise a sack of coal for their hut!'

I trust they were more successful than Keith Hopkins, who recalls crashing into another cyclist when they were both on a similar mission to sneak some extra coal from the Camp store for their huts.

Joan recalls how the WAAF MT drivers handled a wide range of vehicles including three-ton lorries.

> 'We had to do a daily inspection on the vehicle we were scheduled to take out. This meant checking petrol, oil and water. In the cold weather there was anti-freeze only for the fire tenders and ambulances, which meant that other vehicles had to be drained off at night. It was no fun filling them the next morning with water from a tea bucket as, if it split, as they often did, the plugs got wet and it was a problem to start the vehicle.'

The cold weather was also responsible for further extra work as Joan knows only too well,

> 'If on a night duty with the temperature below zero the vehicle would have to be run up every hour.'

Many relationships blossomed between the men of OTU and WAAFs and numerous marriages resulted. Denise Cramp met her husband at Wing, as indeed did Joan Greenacre and no doubt the weekly hops at Wing Village Hall brought many other couples together. These dances were obviously very popular and it can be imagined that the Hairdresser's on the Site was a busy place, especially popular from August 1944 for this was when it received a hooded dryer. The ORB records the moment making the statement,

> 'Far more airwomen will now be able to pass through the hairdresser's daily.'

On the subject of hair Joan Greenacre has a distinct memory of

> 'the sight in the huts after 'lights out' at 11pm as numerous girls would be sitting up in bed putting curlers in their hair by the light of a candle and the FFI inspections (Free From Infection) of hair on return from leave.'

By all accounts life was reasonably harmonious in the WAAF huts. Joan suggests that

> 'the girls got on well together, as not only did we work together but we also had to live together in the same hut.'

However, it seems that there were times when things did not go quite so well, particularly in June 1944. It was then that the Unit was involved in an Establishment experiment which

Romance blossomed at the Unit. The wedding of Jock Frew took place at All Saints Church, Wing with the best man Flight Sergeant Sadler. Amongst the guests are WAAFs, airmen and the best man's son Derek. (D.S.)

moved the WAAFs around different Units rather than them staying at one Unit for a longer period of time. The result of this is recorded in the ORB.

> 'It has been a dreadful month. Approximately eighty airwomen have been posted out and ninety six posted in between the 1st and 11th and with further movements since. These mass postings have caused considerable repercussions, the most difficult to combat being a wave of discontent amongst the airwomen. Many of the nicest airwomen have been posted and the replacements are of a very poor standard.'

Thankfully, following this upheaval and quite possibly the ending of the experiment things returned to normal and a 'happier spirit' is recorded.

To maintain morale, 92 Group Bomber Command organised a competition between the WAAFs at the various Units, covering a wide range of topics. Proudly, in 1944, 26 OTU gained 2nd prize in what was known as the Sunderland Cup.

As with their male counterparts the women enjoyed a variety of sporting opportunities including netball,tennis and hockey and there was also a women's cricket team. Joan Greenacre remembers that tennis balls were in short supply but at least the generosity of one Wing resident enabled tennis to be played. This was a Mrs Tatham who allowed her courts to be used by personnel from the airfield.

Another vital role played by the WAAFs at Wing was welcoming home the former Prisoners Of War during April and May of 1945. An article in Picture Post of May 12th 1945 includes photographs taken at an unnamed airfield showing just such a scene as a plane arrives. Pat Richards has been able to confirm that these were taken at Wing as she recognises some of the girls featured in the photos, particularly a Sergeant Brown who worked in Administration.

The reporter commenting upon the events was Macdonald Hastings and his words depict a most poignant moment in the history of Wing airfield.

> 'The welcome by the personnel of the RAF Station was the most quietly touching thing I've ever seen. As the aircraft ran up to the hangar, there was waiting the one thing these men needed to see more than anything else in the world – a crowd of English women. And as each got off the aircraft, he fell into the soft arms and heard the gentle welcoming voice of a girl who grabbed his bag and walked hand-in-hand with him into the hangar.'

These returning ex-pows had good reason to remember the WAAFs at Wing but the contribution of the WAAFs is quite rightly long remembered by all who were at 26 OTU.

CHAPTER 15
Visitors

Although an infrequent occurrence, it was not uncommon for Wing to receive aircraft returning from operations, that had been diverted from their own base due to adverse weather conditions or were suffering engine problems and required a runway to land on. On the 23rd January 1943, for example, those at the airfield witnessed the arrival of a B17 Flying Fortress that was unable to reach its base at Chelveston near Rushden due to the combination of a shortage of fuel and poor weather conditions there. It was even more exciting at Little Horwood, however, where thirteen B17s found a safe haven. All had returned from an operation on Lorient, with aircraft number 122504 staying on at Wing into February for repairs. Not all arrivals in such circumstances landed safely, with probably the most memorable incident being that involving another B17 Fortress numbered WWX 42-3449 that came down in the Kemsal Wood, on the opposite side of the Wing to Stewkley road to the main runway. This particular crash took place at 2015 on 23rd September1943 and Fred Capron remembers it well.

> 'I recall remarking to a colleague in the twilight of a September evening that the aircraft – with headlights on – was approaching too low. There was the sound of a crash and we all hurried to the spot. One engine sat on a broken tree stump as if placed there. All the crew survived.'

His memory of the engine on the tree stump is accurate as the remarkable photograph taken by one of the crew clearly shows.

What makes the incident even more memorable is the fact that the pilot of the USAAF B17 was 25 year old Major Immanuel J. Klette, who, after recovering from the injuries sustained in the accident, went on to complete 91 combat missions, the greatest number flown by any USAAF pilot during World War II. Klette who was to rise to the rank of Lieutenant Colonel and receive many awards including the military's third highest award for gallantry, the Silver Star, wrote in a letter to the late Peter Bond of Ascott dated 31.10.1984,

> 'We had bombed a Nazi submarine supply ship after sunset in Nantes Harbour and were returning to Thurleigh. I was losing petrol and had to turn over the lead of my formation to my deputy. The RAF gave me a steer to an aerodrome which I later learned was Wing, but we didn't have enough petrol to get there.'

The story continues....

This was Manny Klette's 28th mission and on reaching the target in the late afternoon the aircraft was hit by exploding enemy flak, a fragment of which damaged Klette's left shin bone and in addition had smashed the bomb bay doors, making it impossible for them to be closed, thus causing drag on the bomber. On leaving the target, it was found that fuel was being lost, as

The engine from the USAAF B-17 bomber that crashed into Kemsal Woods on 23rd September 1943. It is sitting on a tree stump some 50 yards from the main body of the aircraft as if it had been carefully placed there. (G.Bo.)

one of the petrol tanks had been holed and an automatic self sealing device had failed to activate. It was now evident that number 2 and 3 engines would have to be shut down, and as they neared the English coast they realised that to return to Thurleigh would be impossible.

The aircraft was now losing height rapidly and with the fuel situation becoming even worse, a decision was made to shut Number1 engine down also. The stricken B17, now with only one engine, approached Wing village.

As Manny Klette himself recalled,

> 'I vividly remember seeing a series of small gulleys into which WWX was headed. My air speed at that point was about 130mph, enough for me to raise the aircraft nose from certain disaster and land in the forest.'

With powerful landing lights on, in the gathering dusk, the aircraft with its fuel finally exhausted came to rest in amongst the oak trees. As the 20 ton bomber came crashing down through the trees, one large oak severed the left wing and broke the fuselage in half behind the radio room. The crew of nine all escaped with their lives, but not without serious injury. Manny Klette had five fractures, and his navigator Lt Madden who was trapped in the nose of the bomber suffered eight fractures. They were quickly taken along with one other crew member to RAF Hospital Halton and later to the Churchill Hospital in Oxford.

Manny remembered,

> '..the squared ambulance...and telling them that my navigator and I both needed morphine shots to deaden our pain, and these being promptly administered.'

John Thornton also recalls the incident,remembering that he and Morris Roberts were both very soon on the spot, and how..

> 'it was very difficult getting two of the crew out. One of the engines was on fire though there was no danger of worse fire because the fuel had run out.'

Manny Klette later wrote,

> 'My bombardier 2nd Lieutenant Arthur Isaacs (who incidentally took the photographs) visited me in RAF Halton and mentioned that the Station Commander was perturbed that I had demolished his shooting preserve!'

Following his release from hospital Manny Klette joined the intelligence division at Bushey Park before being reinstated to flying status during the first half of 1944, from when his amazing career continued. He died in 1988 just two days before his 69th birthday and was buried with full military honours at Arlington Cemetery.

The arrival at Wing of B17 Flying Fortresses continued on New Year's Eve 1943 as George Bignell remembers,

> 'I was Sergeant on duty and had a message to say that there were six Fortresses coming in. As we were the nearest airfield able to take them it meant we had to find billets for 50-60 crew for the night whilst the aircraft were refuelled for take-off the next morning.'

The aircraft included 237779B, 2298837A, 239898A all based at Bassingbourn, 239958 and 758K from Podington and 4230155E based at Chelveston. (It may be that each number should have a 42 prefix).

This should not suggest that the only aircraft diverted to Wing belonged to the Americans as Fred Capron recalls.

> 'One remarkable arrival was a Stirling which landed safely enough. On inspection it was apparent that the tail and rudder had been hit by flak as had also been the rear gun turret which was hanging off like the door on one hinge. The rear gunner had apparently baled out safely but extraordinarily his flying boots were still inside the now open ended aircraft. We theorised that he must have felt that if he ever had to bale out, his flying boots in the restricted space of a gun turret would impede him so he took them off. If that was his theory, it worked!'

This could well have been the Stirling of No.75(N.Z) Squadron that landed after jettisoning its bombs in the Cheddington area on 9th April 1944. John Thornton also recalls a Stirling arriving at Wing but overshooting the runway and finishing up removing two roadside hedges on the Wing to Stewkley road.

B-17 WWX 42-3449 as it came to rest in Kemsal Wood 23rd September 1943. (G.Bo.)

'There she lay in a lame heap when I went to fetch the cows in for milking. An RAF Regiment guard was in attendance and seemed glad of my company. The front turret had ripped clean away, but the gunner had not been in it, so all the crew got out safely to tell the tale. What was so impressive was the efficient arrival of a mobile crane. In two hours she was separated in portions, loaded on low trailers and gone.'

Others hoping for a trouble free landing were not necessarily so fortunate as Peter Bond witnessed, when a youngster, on 31st December 1942.

'At 2320 hours, Wellington 1C DV 764, of 11 OTU on a night training exercise developed engine failure, lost height and got into difficulty. In an attempt to land at Wing airfield it approached the village from Ledburn, between Lower Ascott and the South side of Tythe Yard (Toy Yard) Spinney. It proceeded over Rothschild Road at roof top height, removed the top of an elm tree in the front garden and part of the roof of 26 Stewkley Road occupied by Mr. and Mrs. J. Smith and their daughter Ann, all of whom were unhurt. The bomber then crashed in a field half way up Burcott Hill. The crew of five survived but were detained in the RAF Hospital, Halton with the rear gunner sustaining serious injuries.'

The crew members were, Sergeant A.J. Thomas – Captain, Sergeant H.A. Stewart – Navigator, Sergeant R. Boxhall – Wireless Operator, Sergeant L.P. Dennis – Front Gunner, and Sergeant L.H. Farquhar – Rear Gunner.

During June of 1944 the airfield was particularly busy receiving aircraft returning from operations that were diverted for a variety of reasons. On the first of the month twelve Lancasters arrived with another five landing at Little Horwood, whilst on the 6th and 7th fifteen Halifaxes landed at Wing.

Eddy Collyer had been a Flight Mechanic(Airframes) at 26 OTU early in 1943 and remembered a Halifax coming in and remaining at dispersal for some weeks with its interior littered with propaganda leaflets. By the end of the year he had become an engineer flying in Halifaxes and ironically was himself diverted to Wing on 19th December following operations on Stuttgart whilst with 425(RCAF) Squadron. He was happy to arrive safely albeit on three engines, having suffered,

'very heavy flak and the company of fighters.'

On the 19th March his flight log records a similar experience, being diverted to Wing yet again after a similar raid although on this occasion electric storms and icing were the cause. Eddy recalls this visit to one of his old Units,

'I remember an outing to the village pub and writing our names on the ceiling in one of them.'

Whether his companions included the Captain on both these flights, Pilot Officer Lascaille, is not known, but they appear fortunate to have escaped lightly when,

'after visiting the local chippy the Station Commander's car drew alongside and we were ordered back to camp. We were improperly dressed with no hats, flying sweaters and flying boots and generally untidy, but one does not argue with Station

Commanders and we made off towards camp. On the way we ended up at the pub until closing time. Next morning the Station Adjutant understood our predicament and no further action was taken. We took off on three engines and returned to Yorkshire.'

Other unfortunate accidents concerning visiting aircraft are recorded in the Unit's Operations Record Book, including that which saw a Miles Master (DL 484) crash with the pilot, Sergeant Wadden from RAF Croughton, losing his life and another in which an Avro Anson (DG 864) from RAF Millom was involved in an accident, thankfully without loss of life. The arrival of diverted planes, however, was on a small scale compared with the number that arrived during May of 1945.

CHAPTER 16

1944 and all that

The year began with yet more Nickel raids over France, the first covering the towns of Compeigne, Creil, Laon and Espernay on 2nd January. These sorties continued throughout the early months of the year and the ORB praises all the navigators who were involved on the 27th/28th January, describing them as the best ever since Nickelling began at the Unit. Singled out were F/O W.G.Mayles and F/O R.I.Gillies.

The Unit's strength at this time stood at 37 Wellington Mk III, 17 Wellington Mk X, one Anson, four Martinet Mk I, two Oxford Mk II, two Proctor, two Tutor and one Cygnet aircraft with six Tomahawk aircraft assigned to 1684 Flight.

Training continued at pace with Courses 40 and 41 commencing at the start of the year.

February saw further aircraft diverted to Wing and Little Horwood following operations with 13 Halifaxes and one Lancaster landing at the former and five Halifaxes at the latter during that month. Also arriving was a Fortress (238073) from USAAF Glatton. This had been involved in operations and on return an error in navigation required it to make a landing at Wing. The sight of diverted aircraft became quite frequent as the first six months of the year progressed.

There was good news for those billeted in Sites 6-11 when, following a visit from Air Ministry surveyor Mr Froggat, it was decided that water borne drainage, lavatories and ablutions would be installed. Those occupying huts in Sites 4, 5 and 12 already enjoyed such luxuries and this desirable improvement was undoubtedly looked forward to by the residents.

Further good news was received by the MT Section, where the serviceability of vehicles described as prime movers was regarded as of a very high standard. This was especially pleasing considering that there was some difficulty in obtaining spares, particularly for the highly technical vehicles.

In March Group Captain R.M. Coad was appointed Station Commander and he was able to observe the ploughing of land by Unit personnel on the Stewkley side of the airfield. Some 60 acres of land was now used for food production within the boundary of the Station.

The development of the airfield also continued with the construction of the BI Hangar and the Radar Workshop.

An incident in April saw a Stirling from 75 New Zealand Squadron land at Wing en route to a raid over Lille. The aircraft was forced to jettison its bombs in the Cheddington/ Marsworth area which required bomb disposal action from the Station. Fortunately all the aircraft's bombs were located within twenty four hours.

Another unusual incident occurred on 20th April when danger to flying was caused by a barrage balloon which had broken away from its mountings and become stationary over Wing village. The problem was soon overcome and allowed the six recently arrived Hurricane aircraft to begin their new lease of life with 1684 Flight despite the fact that there was some difficulty in obtaining spares for these. The aircraft had the following serial numbers – LF689, LF739, LF757, LF761, LF764 and LF772. April also saw the formation of the 92 Group Screened Instructors School at Little Horwood with a view to ensuring a more uniform and higher standard of instruction by potential instructors in navigation and signals subjects. They were joined in July by the Navigation Instructors School.

A major change occurred in August when the Unit's state was reduced by a quarter. This resulted in Little Horwood being evacuated apart from the four aircraft of 92 Group Communications Flight (which had been stationed there since September 1942) and a small holding party awaiting instructions. The majority of Little Horwood's personnel were accommodated at Wing whilst 1684 Flight was disbanded. However the reduction proved only temporary, with the Unit returning to full strength in October both at Wing and at Little Horwood where flying resumed. However 1684 Flight was not to return.

By November the Unit had 54 Wellington aircraft on strength plus six Hurricanes and two Masters. Two Warwick MKII aircraft (HG349 and HG350) were also to be seen in the crowded skies above the locality as they were being tested at Wing with a view to them being employed for OTU flying if successful. The two aircraft remained at Wing for nearly a year although George Bignell recalls that 'they were not really considered suitable for the job.'

Other arrivals in November were to be seen firmly on the ground. These took the form of Italian co-operators who became a familiar sight at a number of OTUs where they assisted with a range of manual work such as gardening, road maintenance and general building and sanitation jobs. They were housed in Number 6 Site with their own kitchen and NAAFI facilities and presumably the new lavatories!

The 26 OTU Electrical Section photographed at Wing in April 1945. In the back row third from the left is Ken Barrington and standing to his left is John Howitt. (M.T.)

CHAPTER 17
Operation Exodus

One of the most remarkable periods in the airfield's history, possibly even its greatest claim to fame, was when it was selected in April 1945 as a repatriation centre for returning prisoners of war in the exercise named Operation Exodus.

It was on the 9th April that Group Captain Marples the Station Commander issued the following Order Of The Day.

> 'Now that the Allied Armies are advancing into Germany, prisoner of war camps are being overrun and British, Dominion and Allied prisoners of war are being released in thousands. In order to get them back to their homes, or where necessary to hospital at the earliest moment, they are being flown to England from front line airfields as fast as transport aircraft can be made available. Wing has been selected as one of the airfields at which they will land, and from here they will be taken to Reception Camps by Army transport, after a brief medical inspection and some refreshment. The first batch will arrive tonight, and for the next two months we may expect very large numbers any day. There is no need for me to tell you the condition, both physical and mental, in which some of them will arrive, and they will appreciate anything we can do for them. It is our duty and privilege to do all we can to make them comfortable and happy during the short time they will be at Wing, and, although it will mean extra work and long hours for some of us, I know I can rely on all ranks to do their utmost to help. This subject is not to be mentioned to anyone outside the Station.'

That first day saw the arrival of 819 men in 33 Dakota aircraft and throughout the months of April and May thousands more prisoners of war savoured their return to freedom with their feet touching British soil again, at Wing. No doubt many wondered if such an occasion would ever happen and their feelings of joy and relief must have been overwhelming, as Hugh Lynch-Blosse testifies in his book, 'Wings – And Other Things'.

> 'My party was flown to Brussels and from there to Wing where I got the biggest thrill of my life when I stepped out onto England and walked into the hangar – what a welcome; it nearly made me weep.'

George Bignell makes a similar observation as he recalls,

> 'Some of the returnees had tears in their eyes at the sight of the WAAFs for it had been so long since they had seen a woman. Some gave the WAAFs all sorts of gifts although the CO put a stop to that when he found out.'

The busiest day was the 8th May on which some 1750 prisoners of war arrived, whilst the

15th saw no less than 132 Lancasters land.

> 'The aircraft were coming in so fast, the runways were full. They were landing before the one in front had got to the end of the runway.' – George Bignell.

John Streeter was also at Wing at this time and remembers,

> 'It was just like a modern day major airport – those air traffic controllers certainly had a busy time.'

George Bignell recalls how one of the hangars (Hangar 2) was prepared to receive the men on arrival.

> 'It had been fitted out into different sections so they could be sorted into groups by nationality.'

The condition of those returning no doubt left a marked impression on those who witnessed the arrivals.

Fred Capron can still picture,

> 'some in uniform or a variety of uniforms and some just in blankets. They were de-loused, had a simple medical and were interrogated.'

John Streeter has the memory of,

> 'meeting them at the aircraft with what little kit they had, then meeting them in the hangar after they had been de-loused and getting them a cup of tea. We would have a chat until the transports arrived and then it was out to greet the next lot.'

George Bignell remembers,

> 'We had to prepare the machines ready for spraying the men with all sorts of powder to kill off the bugs and fleas.'

This aspect was not forgotten by Hugh Lynch-Blosse who describes the welcome laid on at Wing.

> 'It was almost midnight as we walked into the hangar, a week under 50 months since my crew and I had taken off from Alconbury on our ill-fated sortie. The first thing that happened was that we were sprayed with DDT! Emerging from the de-lousing room into the main part of the hangar we were met with a sight few of us will ever forget mostly because it was so unexpected. The hangar was decorated with flags, bunting, balloons, flowers, coloured lights and a large number of delectable young WAAF ladies. The band was playing, there was food and drink in abundance, and warmth and smiling faces were everywhere. Anyone who has not seen these things or heard the softness of a woman's voice for several years will be well aware of the emotions that flooded our minds.'

One amusing story told locally concerns a Cublington man name Brazier who was a returning prisoner of war and who, when he asked where they were landing, was told – 'Wing'.

> 'That can't be right,' he said, there is no airfield at Wing!'

Obviously it was during the time he was held captive that the airfield had been built, so he must have been quite surprised when he discovered that it was indeed that Wing at which he was landing. The story continues that the man was allowed to visit his home just down the road before being taken to London.

By the end of the operation a staggering 32,822 men in an equally amazing 1269 aircraft had landed at Wing during those two months. The following extract from the ORB sums up the position and lists the numbers of personnel returned to Wing and their nationalities.

With so many aircraft arriving in rapid succession it is perhaps surprising that there were so few accidents or near misses. One aircraft that did encounter a problem was a Lancaster that suffered a burst tyre on coming in to land.

> 'It came in across the grass nearly to the Watch Tower, but the pilot opened his starboard engines full throttle to turn the aircraft round and stop. The POWs just got out cheering and shouting, not realising how near they had been to a disaster.' – Fred Capron.

Soon after and more seriously another Lancaster came in with one engine on fire but the fire crew managed to control it before it spread. John Streeter witnessed that incident.

> 'It finished up at the end of the runway and I remember seeing bods running from all directions towards the aircraft ready to help. I did hear that one engine had torn away from the wing mounting.'

On 3rd June, with official notice having been received that the airfield had received its last intake of POWs, Group Captain Mangles, in the Order Of The Day, congratulated everyone at the Station on their marvellous efforts, as follows,

> 'On 9th April, before the first ex-prisoners of war arrived at Wing, I issued an Order of the Day telling you the plan for repatriation as far as I knew it at the time, and calling for your co-operation and help in receiving them. Within a few hours of writing that order I realised that all of you were determined to give these men the splendid reception they deserved, no matter what it cost you in lost leisure or sleep. Between 9th April and 18th May, 1,269 aircraft carrying 32,822 ex-prisoners of war landed at Wing, and although this often entailed working on into the night and long hours of waiting, your enthusiasm and determination to give them a warm welcome never flagged. During this period many officers, many of very high rank, came to see how these ex-prisoners of war were being received, and all of them expressed their admiration and pleasure at the excellence of the organisation and the spirit of the reception. Now, after a disappointing fortnight in which no ex prisoners of war have arrived, but during which we have been kept standing by, I have now had official notification that no more will be arriving at Wing, as almost the last of them has been repatriated from Germany. But I cannot let this (matter) in the history of the Unit close without thanking you for making this arduous though very pleasant task, a resounding success. I shall not single out any individuals or sections for particular praise as all of you, (out) of Wing and of Little Horwood, whether he or she was working in the (air), on the airfield, in some other part of the Station or driving a vehicle outside it, have played your part magnificently. This is a Unit achievement of which we may be justly proud, and which will I believe, long be remembered by those who passed through.'

How prophetic were the words in that final sentence as the memories of those involved testify. One of those to return to Wing was Harry McLean, who had undertaken his training at 26 OTU in 1942 and had since completed 25 Operations.

Another interesting tale is told by WAAF Joan Greenacre (nee Webdale).

> 'Amongst one lot of POWs to return was a crew from Wing. I believe they went too far over the North Sea on a Night Cross-Country flight. I remember well (as an MT driver), having to wait for their return or for news of them long after night flying had finished. Finally, they were given up and posted missing.'

This could well refer to the crew of Wellington 1C HE 855, piloted by Sergeant D.J. Morley, that was indeed reported missing on one such training flight on 25th November 1943. If so, no doubt they were delighted to be back at Wing, even though it was a year and a half later than they might have expected!

The whole operation was a great success and, as with any aspect relating to the period, stories of courage and coincidence abound.

Bob Soutar RNZAF, who was at Wing as a Pilot Instructor, returned later when piloting a Lancaster during Operation Exodus. His story concentrates on the coincidence factor, but there is no doubt that the courage element could also be brought to the forefront.

> 'When I was in New Zealand training in Tiger Moths, I roomed with another trainee called Frank Penman. I volunteered for further training in Canada whilst Frank opted to get his Wings at home. We met again in Canada and later travelled across to England in the same troop-ship, 'The Empress Of Asia'. There we parted and the next news I heard of him he was reported 'missing', although soon after I discovered he was safe. I discovered that he had flown a Wellington out to Egypt but got lost and crashed in the desert. As a result of contracting diphtheria Frank was shipped back to England on the liner 'Laconia', which got caught in the South Atlantic by a U-Boat, was torpedoed and sunk. Frank survived and was rescued and taken as a prisoner of war. On May 4th 1945, I was sent to Brussels in a Lancaster as part of Operation Exodus and on landing and stopping engines a large crowd of POWs was visible. And there standing right in front of my aircraft was Frank Penman, and I was able to ferry my friend back to England after his three years in captivity – our destination – Wing!'

The following extract from the Unit ORB for May 1945 gives a remarkable break down of the statistics relating to this momentous occasion. Former prisoners of war of 21 nationalities were received from the three services, in a staggering 1,269 aircraft in an operation which must have been truly astonishing to witness.

See picture overleaf.

N.G. | May.

REPORTS FROM SECTIONS.

(1) Station Headquarters.

Priority activities were again devoted to the reception of Ex-Prisoners of War during the month, and all arrangements continued to work smoothly. The zeal and enthusiasm which characterised these operations during April again was evidenced on the part of all concerned. The following is a summary of aircraft and personnel who landed at Wing, shown under their various nationalities and services.

Aircraft.	Personnel.	Sick Detainees.
1,269	32,822	494.

ARMY PERSONNEL.	
British.	21,170
Australia.	960
Canada.	1,032
New Zealand.	949
F. French.	21
Spain.	15
Palestine.	206
Poland.	139
Greece.	8
Malta.	4
Serbia.	1
Russia.	1
U.S.A.	1,308
S. Africa.	1,295
Holland.	6
Cyprus.	283
Belgium.	8
Algeria.	5
Tunisia.	1
Yugo Slav.	2
India.	1,013
	28,727

AIR FORCE PERSONNEL.	
R.A.F.	1,943
R.C.A.F.	458
R.N.Z.A.F.	108
R.A.A.F.	177
U.S.A.A.F.	55
F.French.	3
Yugo Slav.	12
Norway.	17
Poland.	15
Czech.	4
	2,792

NAVY PERSONNEL.	
Royal Navy.	592
Royal Marines.	126
Merchant Navy.	583
	1,301

CIVILIANS.	2

AIRCRAFT LANDED.	
Dakotas	621.
Lancasters	518
Stirlings	117
Ansons	11
Hudson	1
Mitchell	1
	1,269

At Appendix "2" and Appendix "3" are copies of Orders of the Day issued by the Station Commander on 9th April and 3rd June, 1945. 2 and 3.

Copy of the page in the Operations Record Book detailing the numbers of ex prisoners of war who returned to the UK via RAF Wing as part of Operation Exodus in April and May 1945.

CHAPTER 18
1945/46 – The End is Nigh

From January, 60 Group Radar Navigation Aids Test Flight was attached to 26 OTU with two Wellington X aircraft (NA840 and NA841) that were testing the Gee Chain. This Flight remained at the Unit until it was disbanded on 31st October. The first of these aircraft started life at 30 OTU in January 1945 and within a month appeared at Wing where it remained until June, eventually finding its way to 48 Maintenance Unit where it was to stay until being struck off charge in March 1948.

The year brought hectic activity with the return of former prisoners of war, details of which can be found in the previous chapter and it is more than a little ironic that some of these may well have come back to Wing later in the year to form part of Number 81 Course, which was largely made up of ex POWs.

The Station ORB contains far less information at this time in comparison to previous years with only brief details of events such as accidents. As it happens there were also far less of these with June heralded as an accident free month, as indeed were both July and August.

June also saw the disbandment of 92 Group with the Unit becoming part of 91 Group. Also at this time the Americans vacated Cheddington which was returned briefly to 26 OTU on July 12th after which No.1 Overseas Packing Unit was duly formed and was joined by the Road Vehicle Disposal Unit whose role was to handle vehicles in readiness for public auction. The site at Cheddington continued to be used for various activities for some years. Up to April 1946 personnel were accommodated from the Meteorological Signals Centre housed in Dunstable and also from the Medical Training Establishment at Halton. Technical Training Command took over at that date with the site finally being closed as an RAF Station in February 1948. Following closure the site continued to have a military function and was used by the War department for 'secret purposes'.

Training at Wing continued throughout 1945 albeit on a reduced scale, although November saw the last of the flying from Little Horwood.

1946 opened with the arrival of a new Station Commander in Gp Cpt Greig although by this time there was a general winding down as vehicles and equipment began to be transferred to other Units, whilst training was on an ever reduced scale. Course No.82 with seven crews proved to be the last as the proposed Course No.83 was cancelled. It is worth dwelling on the fact that 82 courses took place at 26 OTU, no mean feat, with hundreds of aircrew being trained for their valuable contribution to the war effort. The saddest aspect is that many of them died either in action in the skies above enemy territory or in the numerous tragic training accidents.

In January all operations at Little Horwood were brought to an end and the airfield was passed on to 71 Maintenance Unit on the 15th. Two months later on 4th March 1946 26 OTU was itself closed – the end of an era – even if it was just a short one, lasting four years and two months.

The airfield at Wing was passed on to Maintenance Command on May 4th and used mainly as a storage depot. By late 1948 the Ministry Of Supply started a number of sales at the airfield of a vast range of items and equipment. The catalogue dated 2nd/3rd November 1949 describes the sale as the sixth to be held at MOS Depot number 151 (as the airfield would appear to be called). The sale was undertaken by Messrs.W.Brown & Co of Aylesbury and the many items of miscellaneous government surplus stores and equipment are spread over more than fifty pages in the catalogue. Amongst the vast range on offer were – generators, telephone receivers, forty Indian clinometers, trailers, four crates of blankets, 11 desk lamp shades, eleven 250 volt Wee Meggers(?), 70 crates of knives and forks, one Spenstead dust extractor and sacks of miscellaneous clothing, to name just a few.

Nothing it seems was to be missed during these sales as a note is found in the catalogue stating,

> 'Used or soiled bedding must be sold with the provision that before re-use, the fillings must be processed to conform to the Standard Of Cleanliness required by the draft specification drawn up by the British Standards Institution.'

During the same year the huts on the WAAF Site were made ready for civilian occupation with a view to them being made available to squatters, many of whom were Polish, who had been occupying other buildings on the airfield. Once the buildings were eventually in use Rent Books were issued to the inhabitants to endeavour to secure some revenue.

The airfield continued to be made use of by the authorities with No.282 MU holding an explosives storage depot on the site from April 1954, with the USAF moving in to take over until October of that year. The Air Ministry eventually decided that no further use could be made of the airfield and it was finally sold in April 1960 and returned to agricultural use.

In 1987, land adjacent to the Stewkley Road including part of the runways was purchased by the Faccenda Group Of Companies for the erection of buildings described as a chicken growing unit. The company magazine, entitled Faccenda Focus, in issue 5, July 1987 refers to the site as

> 'Chicken City – an ultra modern place for birds to grow in.'

Most would agree, I am sure, that these birds are not as graceful as the other rather better fliers that once filled the skies above!

By Order of the Minister of Supply — Without Reserve

G R

M.O.S. Depot No. 151

WING AIRFIELD, BUCKS

8½ miles from Aylesbury and 4½ from Leighton Buzzard

Catalogue of Sixth Important Sale

of

Miscellaneous Government Surplus

EQUIPMENT AND STORES

which Messrs.

W. BROWN & CO.

have received instructions

TO SELL BY AUCTION AT WING AIRFIELD

on

WEDNESDAY & THURSDAY

2nd and 3rd November, 1949

Commencing at 10.30 a.m. each day

Certain Domestic Stores will be offered in small quantities

VIEW DAYS: Monday and Tuesday, October 31st and November 1st, from 9.30 a.m. to 4 p.m. each day, and Sale Days from 9 to 10 a.m. each day.

CATALOGUES 6d. each (P.O.'s only) admitting one Person on Sale Days and Two on View Days, may be obtained of the Auctioneers:

Messrs. W. Brown & Co. (Dept. M.O.S)

34, MARKET SQUARE, AYLESBURY

Also at 2, Church Street, Aylesbury; 41, High Street, Tring; 122, High Street, Berkhamsted; and 78, Marlowes, Hemel Hempstead.

G. T. de Fraine & Co., Ltd., Printers, Aylesbury.

Cover of the Sale Catalogue of Equipment and Stores held at MOS Depot No.151 Wing Airfields on 2nd and 3rd November 1949. (J.Pa.)

APPENDIX 1
Aircraft used in Operations 1942

Aircraft No. (all Wellingtons)	Mission date and target						
	30.5 Cologne	1.6 Essen	25.6 Bremen	31.7 Dusseld.	10.9 Dusseld.	13.9 Bremen	16.9 Essen
DV 719	*	*					
DV 821	*	*				*	
DV 867	*	*	*	*	*m		
DV 908	*	*					
DV 823	*	*	*		*		
DV 780	*c						
DV 725	*		*	*		*	*
DV 808	*	*					
DV 825	*	*	*				
DV 723	*	*		*	*	*	*m
DV 707	*m						
DV 871	*	*		*	*		
HX 375	*	*m					
DV 709	*c						
DV 868	*			*			
DV 703	*	*			*		
W 5704	*m						
DV 710	*	*					
DV 740	*m						
DV 721	*	*	*m				
DV 885		*		*	*	*	
DV 915		*			*	*	*
DV 896			*				*
Z 8841			*				
X 9823			*	*			
DV 801			*				
DV 774			*				
DV 941				*	*	*	*m
DV 846				*		*	
DV 822						*	
DV 714						*	*
X 9786						*m	
R 1224						*	*
DV 844						*	
DV 697							*
DV 732					*		*

c – crashed m – reported missing

APPENDIX 2

Further accidents involving aircraft from 26 OTU

Accidents involving trainees were sadly all too commonplace at Training Units and 26 OTU was no exception. Whilst there was always the real threat of losing one's life once involved in operations, it was probably less expected that the training programme would result in so many fatalities.

Whilst it was often the inexperience of the pilot or aircrew that caused the accident, there were many others in which technical problems with the aircraft proved to be the major factor. This perhaps is not so surprising considering that many of the aircraft had been passed on from operational squadrons and were often the worse for wear, whilst others were transferred to and from OTUs with perhaps the more weary specimens being selected.

The following is a substantial list of the more serious accidents, many of which resulted in the loss of life or aircraft being damaged beyond repair. However, it is not intended to be a full list of every accident in which 26 OTU aircraft were involved.

Whatever the reasons for the accidents this list is drawn up in the memory of those young fliers who perished.

6.6.1942 DV 935

This is the first loss of an aircraft of 26 OTU other than those involved in Operations. Whilst at Wing, fire broke out when the aircraft was at standing, probably due to the abnormal heat (86 degrees F in the shade). It is suggested in the Crash Report Card that sufficient heat may have been generated in the front gun turret, which was facing South, to have ignited incendiary ammunition. Following the accident instructions were issued not to use that particular type of ammunition, known as B.Mark 4, in future and to replace it with another, Mk.7, which was not subject to spontaneous ignition. There were no injuries to personnel, although the aircraft was written off.

14.6.42 DV 710

The aircraft crash landed at Cheddington when after practising night landings for 2 hours it failed to climb following take-off. It was considered that after becoming airborne the flap control was knocked down whilst raising the undercarriage with the result that the pilot, Sgt Glover, was unable to maintain height. The pilot's inexperience was considered the cause, although thankfully there were no casualties.

5.8.42 X 9675

When the starboard engine caught fire over Burton Coggles near Grantham, Pilot Officer G.F. Pentory ordered the crew to abandon the aircraft by parachute. It was later discovered that the engine had been running with damaged pistons and fractured con. rods.

Sergeant Phipps, Air Gunner died in this accident.

30.8.42 DV 825

This aircraft had been used in bombing operations as part of the 26 OTU contribution to the Thousand Bomber raids on Cologne, Essen and Bremen. It was to be destroyed in an accident at Cheddington after it lost flying speed and bounced and swung on landing at 1545.

In the Bucks Herald dated 8th January 1943 is a report which reads,

> 'The British Empire Medal (Civil) was awarded to Mr William Miller, Manor Farm, Marsworth and his cowman, Mr Daniel Millins by the King. The award was for the rescue of a pilot and gunner from a crashed and blazing aeroplane.'

Their valiant efforts undoubtedly saved the life of pilot Sgt R.V. McDougal but sadly not that of air gunner Sgt Arnold Hendrikson. He is buried in his home town of Malden, Surrey.

Also during the same period Wellington DV 868, another to survive Operational bombing, was wrecked in an accident at Cheddington, whilst on 6th September at Little Horwood Wellington Z1073 was written off after crashing on landing. There were minor accidents also involving X9823, DV 501 and DV 846 but happily there were no casualties in any of these incidents.

26.9.42 DV 821

This Wellington 1C aircraft had been used in Operations earlier in the year bombing Cologne and Essen as part of the force in the first 1000 Bomber Raids. It had also been one of twelve 26 OTU aircraft to be utilised for the raid on Bremen on 13/14th of September. Having survived the action it was to be destroyed in an accident over Yorkshire where it crash landed with the death of Wireless Operator Sgt Keightly.

9.10.42 Z 1389 (also recorded as R 1839)

This aircraft left Wing on a Bullseye exercise but was not to return. The pilot and his crew all lost their lives as the aircraft crashed possibly in the Cherbourg area of France. The primary cause for the loss of the aircraft was considered to be an error in navigation due in the first place to an aerial lighthouse flashing the letter of another beacon some 65 miles further north. Due to the inexperience of the crew who had only flown one incomplete night cross-country flight they failed to realise the significance of bearing 193 and had poor reception which they failed to rectify. The captain was P/O C. G. Salt RNZAF.

6.11.42 DV 885

Yet another of the aircraft to survive operations but not training. This was written off in a crash caused by engine failure on approaching Little Horwood. Five of the six man crew lost their lives, the one survivor being the rear gunner Sgt Clarke who suffered considerable burns.

Those who did not survive were:

P/O Hugh Murray	–	Pilot
Sgt. John Wilde	–	Bomb Aimer
Flt Sgt Walter Ferguson	–	Air Gunner
Sgt. James Lennox	–	Air Bomber
Sgt. Harry Bailey	–	Air Gunner

7.11.42 Z 1158

The undercarriage of this aircraft collapsed following a heavy landing at Wing airfield. The pilot Flight Sergeant Leddy and his crew were uninjured.

9.12.42 DV 880

This aircraft was damaged beyond repair when a tyre burst on take-off at Wing. The pilot on this occasion was P/O Waugh. The aircraft was previously with 29 OTU.

11.12.42 X 9622

This was the worst accident to involve an aircraft from Little Horwood, when after returning from a night cross-country flight it crashed killing the entire crew.
Those who perished were:

Sgt Edwin Jones	–	Pilot
Sgt Stephen Appi	–	Observer
Sgt William Barclay	–	Navigator
Sgt Eric Clarke	–	Air Gunner
Sgt Donald Bell	–	Wireless Operator

22 12 42 DV 915 (and Z 8950)

Another of the aircraft involved in bombing operations earlier in the year, this was involved in a horrendous collision with another Wellington (Z8950) over Hogshaw bomb range. The screened pilot, P/O Eric Wagstaff was killed as were nine trainees of Number 11 Course. Unfortunately these are not named on the Report documents. The pilot of Z8950 who also died was Sgt Charles Randolph.

One other minor incident reported in December involved Z1444 whose undercarriage collapsed.

13.1.43 T 2619

The accident involving this 26 OTU Wellington 1C took place in Cornwall during cross-country training. The aircraft force landed with its undercarriage retracted after the loss of the port

The crew of T 2619 that survived the crash on Davidstow Moor in Cornwall on 13th January 1943.
Left to right back row: 'Curly' Wragg – bomb aimer, Jeff Harper – wireless operator, John Poynter – navigator.
Front row: 'Butch' Kay – rear gunner, Charlie Belcher – pilot. (J.Po.)

propeller and the partial failure of the starboard engine. The crash report criticised flying control at Davidstow Moor for not giving assistance to an aircraft in difficulty, stating that it may have been able to land safely had the runway been made clear.

The Navigator in the crew was J.C. Poynter and he remembers the incident vividly,

> 'It was our first solo cross-country flight and we had had another Wellington near us going more or less the same way. Butch Kay our Canadian Rear Gunner remarked that the other Wellington had just lost a propeller. He was soon told by Charlie Belcher, our pilot, that the prop was actually ours. Indeed it was, and despite Charlie's best efforts, that plane would simply not maintain height on one engine. Fortunately, Charlie could see Davidstow Moor aerodrome and headed for it, intending to make a single engine landing. This was somewhat hazardous as we plainly had no power to abort and go round again. We could get no radio response from them and as there was an aircraft on the main runway, Charlie had no choice as we were continuing to lose height, but to attempt an even more hazardous cross wind landing on one of the shorter runways. As we approached at about 300 feet, our remaining engine seized up. Now a Wellington without engines glides rather like a brick and we had only a few seconds warning of a crash landing. I was at my table facing to the left in a short corridor past the Wireless Operator with a bulkhead door at the end into the Pilot's compartment. I realised that on impact I was going to go down that corridor like an express train, and managed to put my arm up and take the shock on my shoulder, protected by my flying jacket, parachute harness etc. We hit one of the massive earth banks that pass for a hedge in Cornwall at about 75mph. I sped down the corridor past Jeff Harper, our W/Op, smashed the bulkhead door to bits and blacked out. I think it was only a few seconds before I came to. My first reaction was that I was still alive, then I saw sky above my head and climbed out quickly, for Wellingtons had a reputation for easily catching fire and burning furiously. I was quickly joined by Charlie, Jeff and Butch, but Curly Wragg, (Bomb Aimer), had been in the second pilot's seat and was trapped. The ambulance crew had to release him. Unfortunately, in trying to brace himself he had dislocated his wrist, elbow and shoulder and had to go to hospital. Sadly we were later informed that he had to be replaced in the crew. We slept overnight at Davidstow Moor and the following morning I retrieved my dividers and protractor from the wreckage, before returning to base via a night at the Union Jack Club in London. After a few days leave we had a crew conference and decided that in any future similar circumstances and despite Charlie's first class effort we would not indulge in any heroics to try and save the aircraft, but would bale out. We all agreed we had been very lucky.'

Ironically, it wasn't long before their resolve was once again tested, for the very next month saw another potentially fatal situation confront the crew – see DV 725 5.2.43.

For Wellington T 2619 – T for Tommy – this proved to be the end of an eventful existence with RAF Bomber Command. In a book entitled 'Bomber Command Continues – The Air Ministry Account of the Rising Offensive Against Germany, July 1941 – June 1942', issued for the Air

Pilot Charlie Belcher amongst colleagues on No. 13 Pilots Course – October 1942. (I.C.)

John Poynter with fellow Navigators of No. 13 Pilots Course – October 1942. (I.C.)

Curly Wragg alongside fellow Bomb Aimers of No. 13 Course – October 1942. (I.C.)

Ministry by the Ministry Of Information in 1942, the opening chapter describes a bombing operation and uses just this aircraft as its example.

On the night of 14th July 1941, T for Tommy as it was affectionately known, took off bound for Germany with seven 5001b bombs destined for Bremen. Over the target area the aircraft was subjected to the most intense and accurate light and heavy anti aircraft fire. Two shells struck the aircraft, the first wounding the rear gunner, Sergeant English – a Canadian! It seems the aircraft was soon ablaze and this acted as a signal for further anti-aircraft fire. The pilot, Sergeant Saich, took evasive action but they were soon hit again. The account continues by describing how the aircraft was turned for home in a dreadful state with the chances of a successful return rather slim. Nevertheless with a homeward course set by the Navigator, Sergeant Smitten, the pilot took the aircraft across the Channel. With dry land beneath them the pilot picked out a barley field and on touching down the aircraft swung round but was halted by a pole. The crew emerged without further injury bar bumps and bruises.T for Tommy had flown to safety with a huge hole in its fuselage, with nine feet of fabric burnt entirely away and with half the rudder in similar condition. The pilot and navigator were both awarded the DFM for their efforts in ensuring a safe return.

T for Tommy was obviously patched up and eventually found itself back in the air with 26 OTU, until that fateful day in peaceful Cornwall.

1.2.43 X 9755

This aircraft which had only arrived at the Unit in December was involved in a tragic accident that resulted in four deaths when it crashed at Beachampton after the starboard engine caught fire. Despite considerable efforts by the crew to extinguish the flames the fire was too great and they were unable to prevent the crash. The pilot, Sergeant D.A. McDonald lost his life as did Sergeants McGowan, Donald and Henwood. One crewman, Sgt Hore, survived.

5.2.43 DV 725

The demise of yet another of the Wellington 1Cs used in operations. This aircraft flew on five bombing raids but was damaged beyond repair when it crashed in Cambridgeshire. The crew had only recently survived a life threatening accident in Cornwall and on this occasion the Captain, Sergeant Charlie Belcher and crew were forced to abandon their aircraft, just as they had decided if such circumstances were to arise. The decision to do so was considered to be correct according to the Crash Report. As a result no injuries were sustained. Navigator J.C. Poynter once again recalls the event.

> 'At about 2315 and at 7000 feet an engine seized up and Butch was soon on the intercom requesting permission to bale out. He already had his turret turned athwartships, ready to open the door and go out backwards. The other three of us, bar Charlie, followed through a door beneath the nose. Demmy Dempster, the bomb aimer, had to go first. He understandably needed a little encouragement; after all, looking down into a black hole,

(this being on a night cross-country), is not the most inviting prospect, especially as he had not been with us when we crashed in Cornwall. I duly followed, somersaulting out and pulling the ripcord after a second or so. There was a ripping sound in my ear and for a moment I feared that my chute harness had torn and I made a frantic grab over my head, but it had only been a thin canvas retaining band. I must say that once the chute had opened I felt blissfully happy although of course I could see nothing below me. Suddenly I found myself sitting in a ploughed field. By this time the plane had crashed and was burning a mile or two away, so, after dumping my parachute, I set off to walk towards it. I soon met up with Charlie who had only just managed to get out in time. (As soon as he had let go of the control column the plane went into a spin and lost height quickly). We were finally picked up and taken to RAF Waterbeach and after a sleep and breakfast, Wing sent an Anson to collect us. I can remember being put out at not having a parachute – we were flying too low to use one anyway.'

Despite writing off two aircraft the crew were part of Number 13 Course at 26 OTU, the first Course at the Unit not to suffer any fatalities.

7.2.43 HF 908

After take-off on a dual instruction night exercise the starboard engine of this aircraft caught fire at 500 feet. The instructor took over before the engine cut out completely and being unable to complete a circuit the aircraft crash landed in a field to avoid crashing in Winslow. P/O M.M. Johnstone was injured whilst P/O W.E. Handy was unhurt.

16.3.43 AD 590

In this accident the starboard tyre burst on take-off. The pilot F/O J. Taplin continued with the circuit and made a good touch down but when the flying speed was lost the aircraft swung and its undercarriage collapsed. It was considered that the tyre burst due to it striking an object on the runway. No blame was attached to the pilot.

This Wellington 1C aircraft suffered a collapsed undercarriage on landing at Little Horwood. It had previously seen service with 109 and 192 Squadrons and also 1474 Flight.

11.4.43 BJ 879

At about 0015 whilst flying training circuits, the aircraft was approaching Little Horwood for the third time when it hit the 98ft water tower in Mursley and caught fire. All of the four crew members lost their lives. The Court Of Inquiry stated that the aircraft was so low in its approach that it would not have reached the airfield if the tower had not been there. It also confirms that the water tower, although only some half a mile from the airfield, did not constitute an obstruction.

Memorial to the crew of Wellington BJ 879 which crashed into the water tower at Mursley on 11th April 1943. The picture includes relatives of the deceased crew. (B.S.)

The crew members were:

P/O Dennis Bint DFM, – Screened pilot (i.e. Instructor)
Sgt Francis McHugh – Pilot/Navigator
Sgt Cyril Fox – Wireless Operator
Sgt Joseph Belanger – Air Gunner (Royal Canadian Air Force)

Flying Officer Bint was recorded in the Station Records Book as travelling to Buckingham Palace in November 1942 for investiture of the DFM, along with P/O Cawdron. Sgt Belanger was the eldest of the crew at just 23.

A memorial plaque to those who died was unveiled at a special ceremony held in Mursley to commemorate the 50th anniversary of VE Day.

Johnny Sylvester was duty pilot at Little Horwood that night and gives this account of the incident.

> 'My job was to position myself at the threshold of the runway and as aircraft signalled, by flashing their designated letter on the downwind leg, I would flash back a green if I considered it safe to continue and land, or a red if there was any congestion or obstruction. We had Wellingtons going and returning from exercises as well as doing Circuits and Bumps. Wellington BK 879 flashed his intention to land and I gave him a green all clear. He made a very long and low approach. I watched him getting lower and lower so I warned him by flashing the Aldis lamp. He opened up and gained height and made a sensible touch and go landing. On his second circuit, I gave him the OK to land but he continued to make a low and very dangerous approach, so once again I warned him by flashing the red light. He opened up, gained height and once again completed a successful circuit. By this time I was getting rather concerned and contacted the control tower by field telephone asking them to contact the bomber by radio. The officer in charge told me the pilot was flying dual with a very experienced instructor so I gave the aircraft permission to land. For the third time he made a similar approach and the next thing I saw was a blinding flash in the sky followed by an explosion.'

It seems the impact on the water tower ripped two large holes in the side of the tower although the structure itself was almost undamaged. The ensuing fire left the tower blackened and bent many of the large diameter pipes but within seven days repairs had been carried out and the tower was back in use.

2.5.43 BJ 669

This aircraft was damaged when it overshot on landing at Church Broughton with only one engine operating. During the same period BK 131 survived a minor accident when its undercarriage collapsed although it continued with the Unit until being passed on to 12 OTU where it remained until 7th August 1947. Also suffering a similar accident was BK 553 although this aircraft sustained unrepairable damage.

31.5.43 BJ 977

A somewhat bizarre accident caused damage to this Wellington when it was badly burnt whilst involved in a starting up demonstration. Fortunately the fire was controlled and the aircraft survived.

3.6.43 BJ 776

This accident saw the three crew aboard suffer burns but thankfully survive, when their Wellington III made a forced landing after suffering engine failure. The aircraft landed with its undercarriage up in Clover Grind Field at College Farm, Hillesden. The cause of the engine failure was unknown at the time of the Court Of Inquiry. The Unit Report states that the Wireless Operator and Air Gunner were both taken to Buckingham Hospital after being initially tended by the farmer's wife, Mrs Limes.

The crew members were:

P/O A.P. Vanrenen – Pilot
Sgt E. Crossland – W/Op
Sgt A.C. Mason – A/G

4.6.43 HE 746

Whilst on a cross-country exercise this aircraft crashed at Dumfries with four of the five crew members losing their lives. Only the Navigator Sgt H. Newel survived although he did sustain injuries.

Those of the crew who perished were:

Sgt L. Southam – Pilot
Sgt A. Parker – Bomb Aimer
Sgt G. Mullis – Wireless Operator
Sgt J. Kent – Air Gunner

4.6.43 BJ 647

This proved a tragic accident at Little Horwood when the aircraft stalled on overshooting the runway and crash landed. Sadly Sgt N. Ellacott, the Air Gunner, lost his life whilst the pilot, Sgt L. Butler and Sgt Tilley were injured. The crash report states that Sgt Matthews and three airmen exhibited great gallantry in rescuing the crew from the burning aircraft.

This was obviously a sad day for 26 OTU with five airmen losing their lives in the two fatal accidents. On the same day an incident at Wing saw Y 3926 burnt out at Number 17 dispersal after it had returned from a training flight. It seems the fire was caused by a Verey pistol in the wireless operator's compartment. As the crew had left the plane it seems there was no evidence to actually blame the wireless operator.

8.6.43 BJ 833

In this tragedy, all three crew members perished when their Wellington III dived into the ground, at Sion Hill Farm at East Claydon. The crew were:

Sgt J.P. Calversbert – Pilot
Sgt Geoffrey Fall – W/Op
Sgt Edward Palava – A/G

13.6.43 HE 240

The Crash Report Card states that the pilot Sgt E. Askew on return during night flying exercises, was unable to make the airfield and crashed in a field near the Stewkley Road. In the circumstances it was felt that the injured pilot had 'put up a very good show'.

20.6.43 HE 753

This aircraft crashed on landing and suffered an undercarriage collapse, although the pilot was not to blame according to the Crash Report card. W/O R.F. Huband was the pilot concerned accompanied by P/O C.D. Woodley.

4.7.43 HE 337

This aircraft crashed and burnt out at Wing when it overshot the runway. The pilot Sgt A.J. Donald was considered not to blame however as it appears his co-pilot disobeyed orders.

6.7.43 Z 1684

This Wellington III crashed landed at Little Horwood with the loss of Air Gunner Sgt R. Mitchell. The remaining crew members suffered only minor injuries.

7.7.43 X 3955

Tragedy struck when the aircraft crashed on take-off killing three of the crew and injuring four others.

Those to perish were:

Sgt R. Wynniatt – Pilot
Sgt R. South –
Sgt A.C. Horley –

The Court Of Inquiry stated that the cause of the accident was 'Pilot error of judgement'.

8.8.43 BJ 892

This Wellington III was lost along with the entire crew of seven when it crashed at Miswell Farm

near Tring. The Unit Report states that the Court Of Inquiry found little or no evidence as to the cause. It continues to suggest that the pilot descended below cloud with his engines throttled back to avoid over-revving and stalled, then opened his throttle fully in the resulting dive.
Those who lost their lives were:

Sgt Robert Young – Pilot
Sgt Stanley Morton – Navigator
Sgt Bill Chamberlain – 2nd Navigator
Sgt Kenneth McKenzie – W/Operator
Sgt Anthony Walker – Bomb Aimer
Sgt Ronald Reeve – Air Gunner
Agt Charles Newton – Air Gunner

All are buried in St Michael's Churchyard, Halton.

9.9.43 AH 855

This Tomahawk aircraft was part of the force of 1684 Flight, but when the engine seized on take-off the aircraft overshot the runway, hit a fence with its tyres and landed safely in a field, much to the relief of the pilot, Sergeant A.W.Britten. He was expecting a straightforward fighter affiliation training flight, but thankfully was unhurt in the incident.

A number of minor accidents occurred during the month which resulted in plenty of repair work to the aircraft but no injuries and no actual write-offs. The aircraft involved had the following serial numbers – DF 617, X 3549, Z 1621 and Z 1687

7.10.43 HE 572

Engine trouble forced pilot, F/O G. Balcombe to make a safe crash landing in which no injuries were suffered by the crew. the aircraft however suffered a collapsed undercarriage. The accident happened at Lichfield during a night cross-country exercise. HE572 had previously been with 429 and 432 Squadrons.

11.10.43 Curtis Tomahawk Mk1 AH 781

As with the earlier mentioned Tomahawk this aircraft was part of 1684 Bomber Defence Flight, attached to 26 OTU at Wing. Whilst on aircraft affiliation duty the aircraft stalled onto its back and spun into the ground about a mile from the airfield. The Court Of Inquiry reported that the aircraft was seen to be flying at a low speed at about 700ft. It states that the pilot failed to maintain airspeed after a partial or total loss of power.

Flight Sergeant Herbert Shepherd perished in the crash and is buried in his home town of Urmston.

16.10.43 X 3468

F/O Matmer and Sgt J. Arbury were uninjured when their Wimpey's undercarriage collapsed on landing due to shearing of the top cross tube.

4.11.43 HE 872

Bomb Aimer Harry George recounted his crewing up experiences in an earlier chapter and here describes the tragic accident which broke up that crew.

> 'We started flying together on 25th September 1943 and on our last cross-country flight prior to posting to a Stirling Conversion course we unfortunately flew into cumulo-nimbus cloud and descended rapidly from 16000 feet. With outstanding good fortune we landed safely at RAF Llanbedr in North Wales. The next day our pilot Sgt Les Edwards minus Navigator 'Chick' Chigwidden and myself took off on an air test with the rest of the crew plus two extra fighter pilots who went along for the experience of flying in a Wellington. Chick and I were walking along in Llanbedr when we heard a loud bang and saw a plume of smoke on the hill at the end of the runway. The plane had crashed. Unfortunately Les Humpage, one of our gunners, was killed, whilst the other, Michael O'Hanlon received serious head injuries. Les Edwards had a badly injured arm, whilst the two 'guests', Sergeants Rowan and Frisby were also injured. Les Humpage was laid to rest in Ashton Under Lyne. We discovered later that the aircraft had failed to lift off the ground despite application of full revs and boost and had hit an obstruction and burst into flames.'

Of the first incident at Llanbedr, Harry has vivid recollections.

> 'I was just pinned to the top of the aircraft by the forces that took control of us and then we started a deep dive. This was so steep that anything loose hurtled towards the nose and there was terrific noise from the engines as we careered downwards. Les and I pulled back on the stick to no avail at first, but gradually the rate of descent became more controlled. We broke cloud over water with the plane still refusing to maintain height. So relieved were we that we implored Les to 'ditch it!' but like the ending to a bad dream a runway appeared and as we were perfectly lined up somehow, Les was able to bring her down.'

6.11.43 X 3924

Whilst returning from a Nickel operation on the Pas De Calais this Wellington collided with another LN 295 from RAF Lichfield. The pilot, Sergeant R. Main RCAF was able to make a successful parachute landing but the remainder of his crew all perished. In a bizarre twist the fate of the crew from LN 295 was identical to that of the 26 OTU aircraft.

Those to lose their lives from X3924 were:

P/O D. Potts RCAF – Navigator
Sgt G. Hall – Air Bomber

Sgt M. Grimmins – Wireless Operator
Sgt J. Holbeck RCAF – Air Gunner
Sgt S. Edmundson – Mid Upper Gunner

On the night of 6th November, four Wellingtons from 26 OTU were despatched on a leaflet raid, whilst three others were involved in a night flying Bullseye exercise. It is not absolutely clear as to which this aircraft was involved in. The Crash Report Card suggests that X 3924 was on the Nickel operation whilst Brian Riley who researched the accident and published his findings in 'Air Enthusiast' maintains that both aircraft were involved in the same night flying exercise. Whatever the exercise, the crash was appalling, with debris from the aircraft strewn across a field near the small village of Abbots Ripton near Alconbury. A sizeable crater had been made by the impact as X 3924 hit the ground. The other aircraft, from 27 OTU actually came down a few miles away near the village of Brampton.

Sergeant Main was admitted to the USAAF Station Sick Quarters at Alconbury. He later described his recollections of the incident and these are reproduced from the 'Air Enthusiast' article, with thanks to Brian Riley. It appears that whilst flying north near Huntingdon, Sergeant Main suddenly saw another aircraft in front of him. He pushed down the Wellington's nose but it was too late and he felt the impact of the other aircraft on the port side. He then gave the order to abandon the aircraft and heard the Navigator say, 'OK, get the' chutes'. The aircraft went into a spin to port, then flicked into an inverted spin which threw the pilot out of the cockpit. This was to save his life with only minor leg injuries being suffered on landing. X 3924 had been built by Vickers at Squires Gate, Blackpool and had been first taken on charge by 12 Maintenance Unit before moving on to operational flying with 115 Squadron. It was transferred to 26 OTU on 20th February 1943.

25.11.43 HE 855

This aircraft with seven crew members on board set out on a night cross-country exercise over the North Sea but did not return and was reported missing and although a search party was organised with three aircraft taking part no sightings were made.

What makes the story particularly interesting is that a crew from the Unit was said to be amongst the returning ex-prisoners of war in 1945. It seems they were posted 'missing' at the time after setting out on just such an exercise over the North Sea. However, the Commonwealth War Graves Commission have confirmed to me that the crew of HE 855 are included on the Runymede Memorial. Perhaps another aircraft from the Unit was reported missing in similar circumstances. Alternatively the suggestion that such a crew returned amongst the ex-pows may have been inaccurate.

The crew members of HE 855 were:

Sgt Derek J. Morley – (1396508) Captain
Sgt Albert E. Ford – (1421773) Navigator
Sgt Desmond J. Conroy – (RAAF AUS 418632) Air Bomber

Sgt Kenneth J. Page – (749356) Wireless Operator/Air Gunner
Sgt Lionel G. Pullen – (1258731) Air Gunner
Sgt George B. Mould – (RCAF R193899) Mid-Upper Gunner
Sgt John H. Ashcroft – (1512556) Second Navigator

11.12.43 BK 440

In September this aircraft had taken part in a bombing operation over France without mishap, however during a night training exercise it was damaged beyond repair when it crashed at Hindolveston, near Foulsham in Norfolk. The pilot had earlier in the evening completed a cross-country exercise accompanied by a screened pilot whom he had satisfied as to his competence to repeat the exercise with his crew. The same aircraft was used after refuelling and an inter-flight inspection. The flight commenced at 0045 hours and appears to have proceeded normally for one hour fifteen minutes. The aircraft was then sound plotted by the ROC post at North Elmham proceeding in a North easterly direction at about 1000ft. The inspection discovered that a structural failure had occurred at a comparatively low altitude, whilst there was a trail of fabric extending back over 200 yards. The aircraft had struck the ground at a very steep angle and burst into flames and there was no evidence to show that any attempt had been made to abandon the aircraft. The report concluded that the crash was caused by loss of control followed by a structural failure in the ensuing dive. The cause for the loss of control was not discovered but probably occurred in cloud or icing conditions.
The crew was:
F/Sgt A. Merridew – Captain
Sgt S. Wilson – Navigator
Sgt N. Doherty – Air Bomber
Sgt E. Brown – W/Operator/Air Gunner
Sgt A. Ellis – Rear Gunner
Sgt W. Martin – Air Gunner
There were no survivors.

30.12.43 BK 491

The Court Of Inquiry reported that this aircraft struck the ground after take-off, having gone into a steep turn. It came down at Nash End Farm near Thornborough after taking off from Little Horwood. All crew members lost their lives.
F/Sgt Kenneth Tucker – Pilot – Royal New Zealand Air Force.
Sgt Alfred Sadler – Navigator.
Sgt Alexander Migner – Wireless Operator – Royal Australian Air Force.
Sgt John Lane – Air Gunner.

29.1.44 BJ 978

This aircraft, having survived bombing operations the previous September, was hit by anti-aircraft fire when off course over London during a Bullseye exercise, at a time when enemy aircraft were active. Fortunately the damage was not severe and the aircraft survived and continued in service until 1947.

5.2.44 JA 455

Whilst involved in a cross-country exercise this Wellington X crashed at Fox Covert, adjacent to the Wing to Stewkley Road at 2315 hours.The Court Of Inquiry found that the main fuel cocks had been turned off by the Air Bomber when he should have turned on the nacelle tanks. Four of the crew survived the crash – the pilot, Sgt. E. Bowe, the navigator, Sgt J. Corrigan, wireless operator Sgt B.O'Hare and air gunner, Sgt K. Pierce. Sadly two members did not survive, namely: Air Bomber – Sgt William Kinsman – Royal Australian Air Force. Second Navigator – Sgt James Duguid – Royal Canadian Air Force.

20.2.44 HE 479

Following take-off on a circuits and landings exercise the starboard propeller 'ran away' and although the pilot took the aircraft to 300ft the engine cut, feathered and they belly-landed, only for the friction to cause the aircraft to catch on fire. It was reported that the undercarriage was not lowered until it was too late as the aircraft was at low altitude. A recommendation was made following this accident that a quick lowering device might be appropriate in preventing such accidents. Although the aircraft was written off, the pilot, F/S J.S.Wood and his crew were uninjured. Navigator Edward Eyres' memories of this accident are recorded in the chapter entitled Accidents.

23.3.44 LP 258

The pilot, W/O H.A.Simmons and crew were all killed when the aircraft failed to recover from a dive and crashed into the ground vertically one mile north-west of Hardwick village, Northamptonshire. Apart from the above named Captain the crew were as follows:

Sgt D.M. Smith – Navigator
P/O R.E. Thornton – Bomb Aimer
Sgt E. Crossland – W/Op/Air Gunner
Sgt J.W. Day – Mid Upper Gunner
Sgt J.A.Marsden – Rear Gunner

In 1998 enthusiasts from the Northamptonshire Airfields and Aircraft Research Group excavated the site of the crash and recovered two engines, cylinder heads, bullets and numerous other components. The group intend to display these at Sywell aerodrome.

26.3.44 BJ 754

This Wellington III crashed at Little Horwood airfield when the starboard propeller disintegrated at low altitude forcing the pilot, F/Sgt R. Rodea into a belly landing. It was discovered that a defective joint on the airscrew resulted in one of the blades becoming detached and entering the fuselage causing fatal injuries to the rear gunner who was actually sitting in the second pilot's seat. The Court Of Inquiry considered that the handling of the aircraft was creditable. Sgt Noel Block – Royal Australian Air Force – was the only casualty. Air gunner Allan Hardwicke remembers the incident and how a number of RAAF colleagues gathered Sgt Block's belongings together requesting that they be sent to the RAAF HQ in London. Sgt Block is buried in the Oxford War Cemetery.

12.5.44 MS 483

A somewhat bizarre accident this, as a practice bomb exploded in the bomb bay at 10,500ft, causing the aircraft to burst into flames. Thankfully the crew of five baled out successfully and there were no casualties. Apparently the last crewman left the aircraft at 400ft. The pilot was W/O R. Mansell and his co-pilot was W/Cdr R. Cook.

The incident occurred over Grendon Underwood.

16.5.44 HF 519

Six crew members including the captain F/O A. Tilton RCAF lost their lives in this tragic accident one mile north west of Llanrwst, North Wales. The crew were on a night cross-country training flight when the aircraft stalled and dived into the ground at a steep angle. The pilot was unsure of his exact position and in attempting to get a visual fix broke cloud but the aircraft stalled as he attempted to clear the surrounding hills.

7.7.44 LP 314

The entire crew of five were killed when the starboard engine failed and the pilot lost control during a circuits and landings exercise. The pilot was F/S J.P. Dalton. The accident occurred in a cornfield within the station bounds at 0215 and wreckage was scattered over a wide area amongst the tall corn. Two of the crew were taken to hospital but died later from their injuries. George Bignell was on the scene of this accident and recounts events in the previous chapter.

9.7.44 BJ 795

In this accident, an engine cut as the aircraft overshot the runway at Little Horwood and hit trees and crashed at Great Horwood. The pilot, P/O Canning was unable to maintain height on just one engine after the starboard engine had failed at 400 feet during a circuits and landings exercise. Four of the crew including the pilot were injured.

A dramatic shot as personnel attempt to extinguish the flames following the crash of Wellington LP 314 in fields close to the domestic sites on the Cublington Road – 7.July 1944. (G.Bi.)

8.8.44 BK 145

Sergeant Wireless Operator Len Land who was at Wing from July to October 1944 recalls being involved in this mishap.

> 'We were just airborne when the port engine failed leaving us with no hydraulics and no air bottle (as there were none fitted) and insufficient altitude to give us time to manually lock down the landing gear. We belly landed on the grass verge beside the runway at Little Horwood and were attended by the Station's crash landing 'facilities' which fortunately were not called into action as there was no fire. A brief spell at Sick Bay proved us all to be suffering a few scratches and shock. The next day we visited the sorry sight of the Wimpy to find her buckled and badly bent and full of earth and rocks.'

The Crash Report Card suggests that the pilot, F/S L.G. Allan was a little slow in ordering the bomb aimer to pump down the undercarriage but does state that 'the pilot did well to avoid loss of life'.

13.8.44 HE 172

This aircraft, piloted by F/S J. Cameron, was to take part in a Night Cross Country exercise from Wing when the accident occurred at 2325. Immediately after take-off the starboard engine momentarily cut and the aircraft swung, struck a tree at a height of 30 feet, crashed and burnt. The aircraft was damaged beyond repair but thankfully the crew survived. There was further concern because the aircraft crashed in the vicinity of the bomb dump and leaking petrol caused a rapid spread of the fire to nearby bushes and grass. The duty and standby fire tenders were almost immediately on the scene and thankfully extinguished the fire before it reached the bays containing bombs and incendiaries. The Station crash tenders located the crew who were suffering badly from shock, burns and injuries and passed them on to the medical orderlies. In so doing, their lives were saved.

3.10.44 LP 254

The crew of five survived this mishap when the aircraft about to embark on Fighter Affiliation training swung on take-off and struck the trees to the south, beyond the perimeter track. Although the wind was reported as gusty, the pilot, F/S W. Stevens was deemed careless. The aircraft was a write off.

26.11.44 NC 654

This aircraft was lost and the crew of five all injured as the aircraft was about to land at Wing. Although the undercarriage was retracted it struck a tree as the aircraft lost height due to feathering in the starboard engine. It appears that the starboard engine was also on fire whilst in flight. As the aircraft crashed it too caught fire and burnt out. No doubt the pilot, F/L Cannell and his crew were mighty relieved to escape.

27.11.44 LP 659

On take-off at 2326 for a Cross-country flight the aircraft swung and crash landed through the airfield boundary. The pilot was criticised for failing to correct the swing by using the throttle. Thankfully he did manage to land the aircraft wheels down and the crew of six were uninjured. The pilot was F/O Skeates.

10.12.44 MF 195

The Crash Report records that this aircraft crash landed with its undercarriage retracted in the 'funnels' at Wing airfield after failure of the port engine at 11500 feet. It also records that the pilot, Sgt H. Hill RCAF, used the wrong emergency call sign 'Empan' instead of 'Mayday' – and there was no answer until the fourth attempt. After the crash the aircraft caught fire in the starboard engine. Only one of the six man crew was injured.

14.1.45 MF 116

This accident occurred at Sketchley in Leicestershire when during a night Cross-country exercise the pilot made a 'Mayday' call after the port engine failed. Sadly the Wellington X crashed with all six crew members losing their lives. The Crash Report indicates that the pilot, Canadian F/O N. Chobaniuk, failed to place the thermal switch in the ON position and was thus unable to feather. It goes on to say that the pilot was also not strapped in at the time of the accident.

3.2.45 HE 574

This aircraft crashed near Whitchurch. The aircraft had previously flown in the Airborne Forces Experimental Establishment, the Royal Aircraft Establishment and 1481 Flight before arriving at 26 OTU. Thankfully there were no fatalities in this accident.

During a night practice bombing run fire was spotted in the fuselage and the crew of six successfully abandoned the aircraft. The accident report states that there was in fact no evidence that any fire had occurred and it was considered that what might have been seen was either the reflection of the upper identification light or smoke which for some obscure reason entered the fuselage.

The pilot F/O G.A. Larder and the crew were given the benefit of the doubt in this instance with no blame apportioned. Surprisingly the Crash report makes no mention of where the aircraft actually crashed.

6.4.45 LN 540 and HE 928

These two aircraft were on bombing practice over Hogshaw Range when they collided following the descent of LN540 through the cloud base. All eleven crew members lost their lives. Of those who died, only the following are listed in the Unit report, F/Lt Marcel Hore DFC – pilot – Royal

New Zealand Air Force. Sgt Derrick Rowson – co-pilot. (Both LN 540), F/Lt Douglas Wix DFC – pilot. (HE 928)

27.4.45 LN 708

There were no fatalities when this aircraft crashed in a field at Redfields Farm near Winslow during Circuits and Landings Training. The pilot, W/O R. Brereton, having decided to 'go round again' was forced to belly land as the port engine failed and height was lost. The Crash Report Card commends the pilot by stating that he 'made the best possible landing'. No doubt his four crewmates agreed. The aircraft however did not survive the crash which occurred at 0225 am. It had previously been with 432 Squadron.

18.6.45 LN 544

Only expert reactions from W/O Edmonds prevented a calamitous accident when this Wellington X began to lose height during an Air Test on the night of 18th June. Dick Revill who was a Wireless Operator Instructor at 26 OTU from May 1945 – June 1946 accompanied W/O Edmonds on this flight and was grateful for his pilot's experience.

> 'There were only the two of us as it was laid down that pilot and wireless operator only were essential to fly in air tests. W/O Edmonds was very experienced and probably flew more hours on Wimpeys than anyone. This was through being seriously injured in 1940 whilst on operational duty. After recovery he flew Wimpeys for the rest of the War in an instructional capacity. On take-off the engine we were testing failed and unable to gain much altitude we dodged wireless masts at the West end of Little Horwood airfield, then flew low over Whitchurch before landing wheels down in a cornfield.'

As a result of this fine piece of airmanship W/O Edmonds was awarded the AFC. Dick Revill had further good fortune later in the year as the details of an accident involving NC446 reveal. (See 13.12.45)

1.8.45 LF 713

Johnny Silvester well remembers piloting this Hurricane during a fighter affiliation exercise.

> 'When the engine suddenly started vibrating, a quick glance at the oil pressure confirmed my fears. No oil. The prop stopped with a loud clunk and after trimming the aircraft into a safe glide I looked for a convenient landing spot. I appeared to be halfway between Wing and Little Horwood and as Wing seemed to be the easiest approach I headed there and was pleased to make a safe landing.'

3.9.45 LP 657

This Wellington X was written off in a tragic crash which killed all five crew aboard during a night Cross-country exercise. On the pupil pilot's first solo Cross-country flight it is presumed he lost control and stalled when trying to pin-point himself below the cloud base as he had been instructed to fly at 2000 feet owing to the cloud at that height. There is some suggestion that the weather conditions were poor enough for such a flight to have been cancelled. As it was, on losing control the aircraft plummeted to the ground. The unfortunate pilot was F/O L. Huygens and the crash occurred at Johnsons Bridge in Lincolnshire.

12.9.45 JA 113

During a night dual circuits and landings run this Wellington X aircraft suffered engine failure and the pilot was unable to maintain height. The pupil S/Ldr P.M. Proctor was forced to crash land in a field some 200 yards from the runway. The Crash Report Card states that on landing fire originated in the port engine and spread to the airframe leaving the aircraft burnt out. One of the crew was injured. The Pilot Instructor was W/O B.Aves. The aircraft had previously flown with 429 Squadron and 17 OTU.

26.11.45 NC 654

Five crew were injured, none thankfully fatally, when this Wellington X crashed just 700 yards short of the runway at Wing. Difficulties arose when the Starboard engine caught fire and although the pilot retracted the undercarriage the aircraft struck a tree on the approach, crashed and burnt out. This occurred on return from a high level bombing training flight. The pilot was F/L C. Cannell.

8.12.45 MW 351

This proved an unusual accident as it involved a Hurricane Mark IIC of 1684 Flight on a Fighter Affiliation exercise. Fortunately both the pilot, F/O C.R. Castleton and the aircraft survived when they belly landed in a field near Wing airfield due to engine failure which caused the aircraft to lose height.

13.12.45 NC 446

Subsequent enquiries failed to determine the exact cause of this fatal crash when during a night Cross-country exercise the Wellington X of 26 OTU plummeted to the ground. All 7 on board, including the screened pilot lost their lives. Dick Revill who survived an accident in June (see 18.6.45) was due to fly in this aircraft but swapped pilots with another Wireless Operator Instructor as they were collecting their parachutes. The crash occurred at Brimpton near Newbury in Berkshire. The screened pilot was F/O Fenwick whilst his pupil was W/O L. Watson.

APPENDIX 3

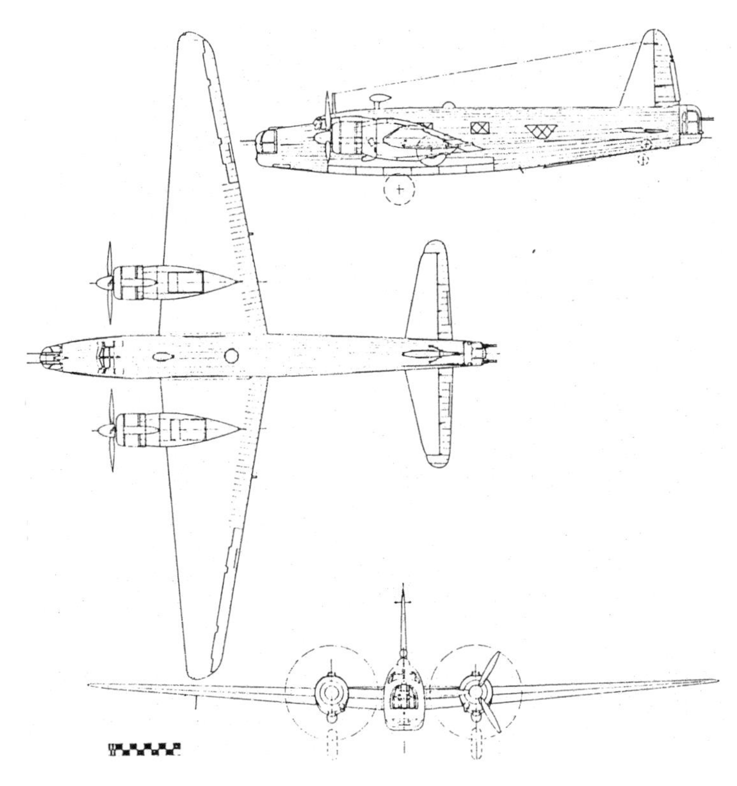

The Wellington Mk X.

Some Notes on the Aircraft used by 26 OTU

VICKERS WELLINGTON

MkIC –	Wing span	–	86ft 2ins (26.26m)
	Length	–	64ft 7ins (19.68m)
	Height	–	17ft 5ins (5.31m)
	Max Speed	–	235mph (378km/hr)

MkIII – as the IC except for –

Length 60ft 10ins (18.54m)

Max Speed 255mph (410km/hr)

The Wellington was affectionately known as the Wimpey after Popeye's friend J. Wellington Wimpey and was the mainstay of RAF Bomber Command until the four engined heavy bombers – the Stirling, Halifax and Lancaster – entered service in great numbers.

The prototype first flew on the 15th June 1936 followed by the first production MkI which was received by the RAF in October of 1938. There were variants of the MkI including the IC which was the model most used by 26 OTU in its early days. This had beam guns replacing the original ventral gun as well as larger mainwheels which protruded from the nacelles when retracted.

The MkI Wellingtons were powered by Bristol Pegasus XVIII engines although later models incorporated the Rolls Royce Merlin or Bristol Hercules engines.

By 1939 Bomber Command had 8 Wellington Squadrons, rising to 21 by 1942 with the aircraft being the first to drop bombs on Germany on 4th September 1939. In May 1942 Wellingtons including a number from 26 OTU made up half of the force for the first Thousand Bomber Raid on Cologne, whilst they were also widely deployed in North Africa, Greece and India.

Further models were developed including the MkIII and MKX both of which were used at Wing, the latter from 1942.

Aircraft used by 26 OTU included those previously attached to Squadrons although with the advent of the heavy bombers Wellingtons were received direct from the manufacturer.

Wellingtons were also in operation with Coastal Command and proved particularly effective against submarines and shipping in the Mediterranean Sea and Indian Ocean.

In total 11,462 Wellington aircraft were built.

AVRO ANSON

Wing span – 56ft 5ins (17.22m)
Length – 42ft 3ins (12.88m)
Height – 13ft 1in(3.99m)
Max speed – 188mph (302km/hr)

This aircraft was a general reconnaissance and aircrew trainer developed initially for coastal patrol duties. The prototype was flown on 24th March 1943 and the Anson entered service one year later as the RAF's first aircraft with a retractable undercarriage.

Nine squadrons were equipped with the aircraft at the outbreak of war and it remained in service in a maritime role until 1941.

From 1940 the Anson found a new role as a navigator, wireless and air gunner trainer and large numbers were built to meet the needs of the Empire Training Scheme. They were, of course, used at 26 OTU in this role.

The last British Anson was built in 1952.

Wellington X PG117 about to take-off at Wing in 1945. The aircraft arrived at the Unit from the Vickers works at Blackpool on 15th February 1945 and was later with 21 OTU and 8 MU. (J.R.)

MILES MASTER

Wing span – 39ft (11.89m)
Length – 30ft 5ins (9.27m)
Height – 10 ft (3.05m)
Max speed – 226mph (364km/hr)

The Master was a two-seater advanced trainer and a modified version of the earlier Miles Kestrel which had been rejected by the RAF in 1937.

The Master however was ordered by the RAF in 1938 and went on to become a standard advanced trainer during the war. It was regarded by those who flew it as having fine flying characteristics and it remained in production until 1942. Not that many were in operation with 26 OTU but there were normally a few to be seen over the skies of Wing throughout the airfield's existence.

MILES MARTINET

This was a purpose built target tug based on the Miles Master II. It first flew on 24th April 1942 and compared to the Master it featured a slightly lengthened nose to compensate for the weight of the target towing equipment which comprised a drogue cable winch powered by either an electric motor or a wind driven propeller. Production ceased in 1945.

AIRSPEED OXFORD

Wing span – 53ft 4ins (16.25m)
Length – 34ft 6ins (10.51m)
Height – 11ft 1in (3.38m)

Another aircraft of which only a few were to be seen at 26 OTU. The Oxford was an aircrew trainer and light transport aircraft commonly known as the Ox-box.

It played an important role in training aircrews in twin- engined flying, bombing, gunnery, radio and navigation skills.

It was first flown in 1937 and entered service with the RAF Central Flying School in November of that year. The various models were designed with particular areas of training in mind; for example, the MkI was a bombing and gunnery trainer, the MKII for navigation and radio etc.

The Royal Australian Air Force and the South African Air Force both used the Oxford for training with over a thousand aircraft involved. A total of 8568 were eventually built upto 1945.

HAWKER HURRICANE

Wing span – 40ft (12.19m)
Length – 31ft 5ins (9.58m)
Height – 13ft (3.96m)

This famous single seat fighter aircraft was used at OTUs after their squadron life was deemed complete and often replaced the Miles Master in fighter affiliation exercises. They were considered to be more like the German fighters in speed and manoeuvrability and therefore a more realistic 'enemy '.

The first production Hurricane was flown in October 1937 and by the outbreak of war just under 500 had been built equipping 18 squadrons. By the Battle Of Britain 659 Hurricane I's were in service in 29 squadrons.

Later models included the Mark IIA, IIB, IIC, IID and Mk IV with the first three being fighter-bombers and the latter two ground attack aircraft.

BOULTON PAUL DEFIANT

Wing span – 39ft 4ins (12.00m)
Length – 35ft 4ins (10.77m)
Height – 12ft 2ins (3.70m)

Another aircraft seen only occasionally over Wing was the Defiant which had been developed as a two seater turret fighter, combining the performance of a fighter with a gun armament in a single dorsal turret.

The concept was not successful, however, with the aircraft's performance and agility affected by the weight of the turret and two man crew.

It first entered service in December 1939 and in its first actions the following May it accounted for 18 German aircraft in a single day although losses were also high. Subsequently the German pilots were quick to learn that the Defiant had no forward firing guns and losses were heavy as a result.

The Defiant was eventually withdrawn from day operations in 1940 and assigned to a night fighting role, with more success.

After 1941 the aircraft was mainly used in secondary roles including that of target towing, which may have been how it was utilised at 26 OTU.

VICKERS WARWICK

Wing span – 96ft 8ins (29.48m)
Length – 72ft 3ins (22.02m)
Height – 8ft 6ins (5.64m)

Two Warwick MkII aircraft were seen at 26 OTU in November 1944 where they were being tested as a replacement for the Wellington. The aircraft had been designed for this purpose as early as 1935 and although trialled over a significant period, it proved unsuccessful. By the time the two aircraft appeared at Wing for continued trials, the decision had been made to adapt the aircraft for air-sea rescue purposes with the first 70 being converted from bombers.

MARTIN-BAKER MB3

Wing span – 35ft (10.67m)
Length – 35ft 4ins (10.77m)
Max Speed – 415mph

This aircraft, a single-engine, single-seat fighter, was designed as an advance on the Hurricane and Spitfire by James Martin. It was to use the then untried Napier Sabre engine and emphasis was laid on simplicity and compactness with the steel tubular structure being extensively covered by detachable metal panels.

Before completion, the prototype was fitted with six 20mm cannon, but these were removed before flying trials began. The aircraft was first flown by Capt. Valentine Henry Baker at Wing on 31st August 1942. The MB3 apparently handled well although the radiator was considered to be unsuitable and the engine temperature rose to 135 degrees Fahrenheit compelling Captain Baker to land after only one circuit. He maintained that too much taxying had caused the trouble and it was agreed that a further flight would do no harm. Again the coolant became excessively hot, boiling after just one circuit, and the aircraft was grounded.

It was felt that some of the problems had been overcome, but then on 12th September 1942, during its tenth flight, the MB3 crashed as Captain Baker attempted a forced landing. The pilot was killed and further development of the aircraft was immediately halted.

The number of DFCs evident suggests that this photo includes a number of Pilot Instructors. It could also include the Commanding Officer but unfortunately no further details are known. It is certain that it was taken at Wing however. (I.C.)

A view of the east side of the Airmen's Dining Room on the Communal Site. (author)

A group of Store Buildings near the Dining Room on the Communal Site. (author)

Some of the remaining buildings on the WAAF Site. These were the ablutions and baths of the Sergeants and Airwomen. (author)

Aerial view of the airfield taken in 1944. Note the Communal Site (bottom centre) with the Instructional Site to its north and the various Dispersed Sites situated alongside the visible Wing to Cublington Road. (I.C.)

GLOSSARY

AA	Anti-Aircraft
a/c	Aircraft
ACW	Aircraftwoman
AFC	Air Force Cross
AFU	Advanced Flying Unit
AOC	Air Officer Commanding
ATC	Air Training Corps.
AVM	Air Vice Marshal
AWOL	Absent Without Leave
BAT	Blind Approach Training
BDT	Bomber Defence Training
BDTF	Bomber Defence Training Flight
Blood Wagon	Ambulance
Bullseye	Exercise carried out by OTU air crews.
Cat.	Category - when relating to aircraft damage.
CFS	Central Flying School
C-in-C	Commander in Chief
Circuits and Bumps	Take offs and landings
CO	Commanding Officer
Corkscrew	Violent defensive action
Cpl.	Corporal
DFC	Distinguished Flying Cross
DFM	Distinguished Flying Medal
DREM	Lighting system of outer markers and approach lights
DSO	Distinguished Service Order
EFTS	Elementary Flying Training School
Elsan	Chemical toilet fitted to many larger aircraft
ENSA	Entertainments National Service Association
Eric	Day training exercise for bomber crews
ETA	Estimated Time Of Arrival

Feint	Name given to diversionary raids by bomber aircraft
Flak	Anti aircraft gunfire
Flt Lt.	Flight Lieutenant
Flt Off.	Flight Officer (WAAF)
Flt Sgt.	Flight Sergeant
F/O	Flying Officer
FTS	Flying Training School
FTU	Ferry Training School
Gee	Navigational aid using ground transmitters and an airborne receiver
Gp Capt.	Group Captain
HCU	Heavy Conversion Unit
HF/DF	High Frequency Direction Finder
HQ	Headquarters
ITW	Initial Training Wing
KCB	Knight Commander of the British Empire
LAC	Leading Aircraftman
LACW	Leading Aircraftwoman
Lt.	Lieutenant
MC	Military Cross
Mk	Mark
MOS	Ministry Of Supply
MT	Motor Transport
MU	Maintenance Unit
NAAFI	Navy, Army and Air Force Institute
NCO	Non Commissioned Officer
Nickel	Operation involving leaflet dropping over enemy territory
Nissen Hut	A tunnel shaped hut of corrugated iron
Operation Exodus	The return of British, Dominion and Allied prisoners of war from the continent to the UK
ORB	Operations Record Book
OTU	Operational Training Unit

PO	Pilot Officer
POW	Prisoner Of War
PT	Physical Training
PTI	Physical Training Instructor
QFI	Qualified Flying Instructor
Queen Mary	Long trailer used to transport dismantled aircraft
RAAF	Royal Australian air Force
RAF	Royal Air Force
RCAF	Royal Canadian Air Force
RNZAF	Royal New Zealand Air Force
RT	Radio Telephony
Sgt.	Sergeant
Sqdn Ldr.	Squadron Leader
SOC	Struck Off Charge
USAAF	United States Army Air Force
USAF	United States Air Force
WAAF	Women's Auxiliary Air Force
Wg Cdr.	Wing Commander
Window	Metallised strips dropped to confuse enemy radar systems
WO	Warrant Officer
WOP/AG	Wireless Operator /Air Gunner
WT	Wireless Telegraphy
YMCA	Young Men's Christian Association

Books Published by THE BOOK CASTLE

CHANGES IN OUR LANDSCAPE: Aspects of Bedfordshire, Buckinghamshire and the Chilterns 1947-1992: Eric Meadows. Over 350 photographs from the author's collection spanning nearly 50 years.

COUNTRYSIDE CYCLING IN BEDFORDSHIRE, BUCKINGHAMSHIRE AND HERTFORDSHIRE: Mick Payne. Twenty rides on and off-road for all the family.

PUB WALKS FROM COUNTRY STATIONS: Bedfordshire and Hertfordshire: Clive Higgs. Fourteen circular country rambles, each starting and finishing at a railway station and incorporating a pub stop at a mid way point.

PUB WALKS FROM COUNTRY STATIONS: Buckinghamshire and Oxfordshire: Clive Higgs. Circular rambles incorporating pub-stops.

LOCAL WALKS: South Bedfordshire and North Chilterns: Vaughan Basham. Twenty-seven thematic circular walks.

LOCAL WALKS: North and Mid Bedfordshire: Vaughan Basham. Twenty-five thematic circular walks.

FAMILY WALKS: Chilterns South: Nick Moon. Thirty 3 to 5 mile circular walks.

FAMILY WALKS: Chilterns North: Nick Moon. Thirty shorter circular walks.

CHILTERN WALKS: Hertfordshire, Bedfordshire and North Bucks: Nick Moon.

CHILTERN WALKS: Buckinghamshire: Nick Moon.

CHILTERN WALKS: Oxfordshire and West Buckinghamshire: Nick Moon. A trilogy of circular walks, in association with the Chiltern Society. Each volume contains 30 circular walks.

OXFORDSHIRE WALKS: Oxford, the Cotswolds and the Cherwell Valley: Nick Moon.

OXFORDSHIRE WALKS: Oxford, the Downs and the Thames Valley: Nick Moon. Two volumes that complement Chiltern Walks: Oxfordshire, and complete coverage of the county, in association with the Oxford Fieldpaths Society. Thirty circular walks in each.

THE D'ARCY DALTON WAY: Nick Moon. Long-distance footpath across the Oxfordshire Cotswolds and Thames Valley, with various circular walk suggestions.

THE CHILTERN WAY: Nick Moon. A guide to the new 133 mile circular Long-Distance Path through Bedfordshire, Buckinghamshire, Hertfordshire and Oxfordshire, as planned by the Chiltern Society.

JOURNEYS INTO BEDFORDSHIRE: Anthony Mackay. Foreword by The Marquess of Tavistock, Woburn Abbey. A lavish book of over 150 evocative ink drawings.

COCKNEY KID & COUNTRYMEN: Ted Enever. The Second World War remembered by the children of Woburn Sands and Aspley Guise. A six year old boy is evacuated from London's East End to start life in a Buckinghamshire village.

BUCKINGHAM AT WAR: Pip Brimson. Stories of courage, humour and pathos as Buckingham people adapt to war.

WINGS OVER WING: The Story of a World War II Bomber Training Unit: Mike Warth. The activities of RAF Wing in Buckinghamshire.

JOURNEYS INTO BUCKINGHAMSHIRE: Anthony Mackay. Superb line drawings plus background text: large format landscape gift book.

BUCKINGHAMSHIRE MURDERS: Len Woodley. Nearly two centuries of nasty crimes.

WINGRAVE: A Rothschild Village in the Vale: Margaret and Ken Morley. Thoroughly researched and copiously illustrated survey of the last 200 years in this lovely village between Aylesbury and Leighton Buzzard.

HISTORIC FIGURES IN THE BUCKINGHAMSHIRE LANDSCAPE: John Houghton. Major personalities and events that have shaped the county's past, including Bletchley Park.

TWICE UPON A TIME: John Houghton. North Bucks short stories loosely based on fact.

SANCTITY AND SCANDAL IN BEDS AND BUCKS: John Houghton. A miscellany of unholy people and events.

MANORS and MAYHEM, PAUPERS and PARSONS: Tales from Four Shires: Beds., Bucks., Herts. and Northants: John Houghton. Little known historical snippets and stories.

THE LAST PATROL: Len Woodley. Policemen killed on duty while serving the Thames Valley.

FOLK: Characters and Events in the History of Bedfordshire and Northamptonshire: Vivienne Evans. Anthology of people of yesteryear arranged alphabetically by village or town.

JOHN BUNYAN: His Life and Times: Vivienne Evans. Highly praised and readable account.

THE RAILWAY AGE IN BEDFORDSHIRE: Fred Cockman. Classic, illustrated account of early railway history.

A LASTING IMPRESSION: Michael Dundrow. A boyhood evacuee recalls his years in the Chiltern village of Totternhoe near Dunstable.

GLEANINGS REVISITED: Nostalgic Thoughts of a Bedfordshire Farmer's Boy: E.W. O'Dell. His own sketches and early photographs adorn this lively account of rural Bedfordshire in days gone by.

BEDFORDSHIRE'S YESTERYEARS Vol 2: The Rural Scene: Brenda Fraser Newstead. Vivid first-hand accounts of country life two or three generations ago.

BEDFORDSHIRE'S YESTERYEARS Vol 3: Craftsmen and Tradespeople: Brenda Fraser-Newstead. Fascinating recollections over several generations practising many vanishing crafts and trades.

BEDFORDSHIRE'S YESTERYEARS Vol 4: War Times and Civil Matters: Brenda Fraser-Newstead. Two World Wars, plus transport, law and order, etc.

DUNNO'S ORIGINALS: A facsimile of the rare pre-Victorian history of Dunstable and surrounding villages. New preface and glossary by John Buckledee, Editor of The Dunstable Gazette.

PROUD HERITAGE: A Brief History of Dunstable, 1000-2000AD: Vivienne Evans. Century by century account of the town's rich tradition and key events, many of national significance.

DUNSTABLE WITH THE PRIORY: 1100-1550: Vivienne Evans. Dramatic growth of Henry I's important new town around a major crossroads.

DUNSTABLE IN TRANSITION: 1550-1700: Vivienne Evans. Wealth of original material as the town evolves without the Priory.

OLD DUNSTABLE: Bill Twaddle. A new edition of this collection of early photographs.

BOURNE and BRED: A Dunstable Boyhood Between the Wars: Colin Bourne. An elegantly written, well illustrated book capturing the spirit of the town over fifty years ago.

OLD HOUGHTON: Pat Lovering. Pictorial record capturing the changing appearances of Houghton Regis over the past 100 years.

ROYAL HOUGHTON: Pat Lovering. Illustrated history of Houghton Regis from the earliest of times to the present.

GIRLS IN BLUE: Christine Turner. The activities of the famous Luton Girls Choir properly documented over its 41 year period from 1936 to 1977.

THE STOPSLEY BOOK: James Dyer. Definitive, detailed account of this historic area of Luton. 150 rare photographs.

THE STOPSLEY PICTURE BOOK: James Dyer. New material and photographs make an ideal companion to The Stopsley Book.

PUBS and PINTS: The Story of Luton's Public Houses and Breweries: Stuart Smith. The background to beer in the town, plus hundreds of photographs, old and new.

LUTON AT WAR - VOLUME ONE: As compiled by the Luton News in 1947, a well illustrated thematic account.

LUTON AT WAR - VOLUME TWO: Second part of the book compiled by The Luton News - with a new index by James Dyer.

THE CHANGING FACE OF LUTON: An Illustrated History: Stephen Bunker, Robin Holgate and Marian Nichols. Luton's development from earliest times to the present busy industrial town. Illustrated in colour and mono.

WHERE THEY BURNT THE TOWN HALL DOWN: Luton, the First World War and the Peace Day Riots, July 1919: Dave Craddock. Detailed analysis of a notorious incident.

THE MEN WHO WORE STRAW HELMETS: Policing Luton, 1841974: Tom Madigan. Fine chronicled history, many rare photographs; author served in Luton Police for fifty years.

BETWEEN THE HILLS: The Story of Lilley, a Chiltern Village: Roy Pinnock. A priceless piece of our heritage - the rural beauty remains but the customs and way of life described here have largely disappeared.

KENILWORTH SUNSET: A Luton Town Supporter's Journal: Tim Kingston. Frank and funny account of football's ups and downs.

A HATTER GOES MAD!: Kristina Howells. Luton Town footballers, officials and supporters talk to a female fan.

LEGACIES: Tales and Legends of Luton and the North Chilterns: Vic Lea. Mysteries and stories based on fact, including Luton Town Football Club. Many photographs.

JOURNEYS INTO HERTFORDSHIRE: Anthony Mackay. Foreword by the Marquess of Salisbury, Hatfield House. Nearly 200 superbly detailed line drawings.

THREADS OF TIME: Shela Porter. The life of a remarkable mother and businesswoman, spanning the entire century and based in Hitchin and (mainly) Bedford.

LEAFING THROUGH LITERATURE: Writers' Lives in Herts and Beds: David Carroll. Illustrated short biographies of many famous authors and their connections with these counties.

A PILGRIMAGE IN HERTFORDSHIRE: H.M. Alderman. Classic, between the-wars tour round the county, embellished with line drawings.

THE VALE OF THE NIGHTINGALE: Molly Andrews. Several generations of a family, lived against a Harpenden backdrop.

STICKS AND STONES: The Life and Times of a Journeyman Printer in Hertford, Dunstable, Cheltenham and Wolverton: Harry Edwards.

SUGAR MICE AND STICKLEBACKS: Childhood Memories of a Hertfordshire lad: Harry Edwards. Vivid evocation of gentle pre-war in an archetypal village, Hertingfordbury.

SWANS IN MY KITCHEN: Lis Dorer. Story of a Swan Sanctuary near Hemel Hempstead.

THE HILL OF THE MARTYR: An Architectural History of St.Albans Abbey: Eileen Roberts. Scholarly and readable chronological narrative history of Hertfordshire and Bedfordshire's famous cathedral. Fully illustrated with photographs and plans.

THE TALL HITCHIN INSPECTOR'S CASEBOOK: A Victorian Crime Novel Based on Fact: Edgar Newman. Worthies of the time encounter more archetypal villains.

ESPECIALLY FOR CHILDREN

VILLA BELOW THE KNOLLS: A Story of Roman Britain: Michael Dundrow. An exciting adventure for young John in Totternhoe and Dunstable two thousand years ago.

THE RAVENS: One Boy Against the Might of Rome: James Dyer. On the Barton Hills and in the south-east of England as the men of the great fort of Ravensburgh (near Hexton) confront the invaders.

Further titles are in preparation.

All the above are available via any bookshop, or from the publisher and bookseller.

THE BOOK CASTLE

12 Church Street, Dunstable, Bedfordshire LU5 4RU

Tel: (01582) 605670 Fax (01582) 662431

Email: bc@book-castle.co.uk

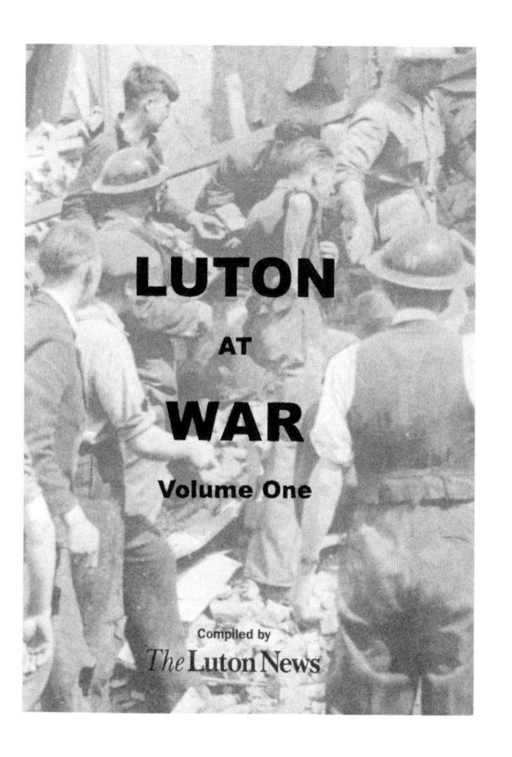

LUTON AT WAR

VOLUME ONE & VOLUME TWO

Initially published by the Luton News in 1947, the story of how the people of Luton withstood the dark years of war between 1939 and 1945.

Because of strict war-time censorship much of what occurred during those years was not mentioned in The Luton News. Once the war was over however, The Luton News set about the mammoth task of presenting a complete and vivid picture of war-time life. It tells of the long anxious nights, the joy and the sorrow that made even the most terrifying moments bearable thanks to the tremendous way in which the people joined to help each other.

Written and compiled by the staff of The Luton News at the time, it contains the most comprehensive and fascinating pictorial record. As well as being a moving personal account it is a unique historical document.

Now published in large format paperback in two parts, it is packed with hundreds of rare photographs. For this edition, a new index has been compiled by James Dyer, appearing in the second book but covering both volumes.

BUCKINGHAM AT WAR

by Pip Brimson

Stories of courage, humour and occasional pathos as Buckingham people adapt to a state of war. How A.R.P., gas masks, blackout and mobilization were all coped with. How the formation of the Home Guard- Land Girls and the jobs women were directed to affected the town. The progress of war through those early years, including rationing and evacuation; the stories told by evacuees in the town. Read about the individual effort by those at home, and the town's fund raising events. When at last the end of the war approached, the blackout was lifted; the Home Guard, their job finished, stood down, and prisoners of war overseas began to return home to great rejoicing, which culminated on V.E. and V.J. Days. Servicemen too, were slowly beginning to demobilize. Finally, everyone could sit back and take stock - attend to their losses and sadness, but feel proud of what had been achieved - and then, begin to prepare for the problems and happiness Peace would bring, after the long years of struggle and endeavour.